Trouble in the University

Studies in Critical Social Sciences Book Series

Haymarket Books is proud to be working with Brill Academic Publishers (www.brill.nl) to republish the *Studies in Critical Social Sciences* book series in paperback editions. This peer-reviewed book series offers insights into our current reality by exploring the content and consequences of power relationships under capitalism, and by considering the spaces of opposition and resistance to these changes that have been defining our new age. Our full catalog of *SCSS* volumes can be viewed at www.haymarketbooks.org/category/scss-series.

Trouble in the University

How the Education of Health Care Professionals Became Corrupted

Mildred A. Schwartz

Chicago, IL

First published in 2014 by Brill Academic Publishers, The Netherlands.

Published in paperback in 2015 by
Haymarket Books
P.O. Box 180165
Chicago, IL 60618
773-583-7884
www.haymarketbooks.org

ISBN: 978-1-60846-495-1

Trade distribution:
In the U.S. through Consortium Book Sales, www.cbsd.com
In the UK, Turnaround Publisher Services, www.turnaround-uk.com
In all other countries by Publishers Group Worldwide, www.pgw.com

Cover design by Ragina Johnson.

This book was published with the generous support of Lannan Foundation and the Wallace Action Fund.

Printed in Canada by union labor.

10 9 8 7 6 5 4 3 2 1

Library of Congress Cataloging-in-Publication Data is available.

Contents

Acknowledgements

This work could not have been completed without help from many sources. Names are listed alphabetically to give equal recognition for their essential contributions. Those who gave me access to information, directed me to relevant materials or individuals, or otherwise helped include Jonathan Bearack, Alex Bernstein, Patrick Egan, Kathy Kleeman, Donald Light, Josh Margolin, David Mechanic, Robert Morris, Ryan Raffery, Rebekah Rasooly, Renee Steinhagen, and Robert Vietrogoski. Colleagues and special friends helped by reading chapters at various stages of completion. They are William Bridges, Edward Lehman, Ethna Lehman, Russell Schutt, Robert Vietrogoski, and Wendy Young. I benefitted greatly from their criticisms and suggestions even though I was not always prepared to accept their advice. The most direct information about how UMDNJ operated came from current and former faculty. I promised all of them anonymity and therefore cannot publically thank them for their willingness to speak candidly about what they had observed.

Writing this book was helped immeasurably by the opportunity to work in the congenial atmosphere of the Department of Sociology at New York University where I enjoy the privileges of a Visiting Scholar. During the academic year of 2012–13 I was a network fellow at the Edward J. Safra Center for Ethics at Harvard University. Regular communications about the activities of other fellows broadened my understanding of institutional corruption and directly influenced the interpretation of my own data.

Special thanks are due to Michael Meyerson who drove me to appointments, accompanied me to meetings, and constantly supported my work, no matter how disruptive to a tranquil life.

CHAPTER 1

The Corruption of Higher Education

Encountering Corruption

After I moved to New Jersey in 1999 and began reading the local newspaper, *The Record* of Bergen County, I was struck by the number and variety of stories about corruption in politics. The issues covered were not unfamiliar to me, a longtime resident of Chicago, but I sensed a different quality from what I knew in my previous home. It appeared that corruption in New Jersey was more a matter of personal gain, with minimal regard for redistributing rewards to constituents or clients. I do not know, in fact, whether this was true or merely an impression but it started me thinking about corruption generally.

An examination of the political science and economic literature revealed the diverse ways in which corruption had been defined. Yet absent from most definitions was recognition of the social and cultural elements that give rise to corruption and shape how it is manifested. Later I would read Granovetter's (2007) concerns about this lack of attention to social factors involved in corruption, but prior to that, I started exploring the possibility of a comprehensive sociological theory of corruption. I had produced an early draft of such a theory when my continuing newspaper reading brought even more troubling news.

The diligence of local investigative reporters, particularly at the Newark *Star Ledger*, led to a continuing string of stories about wrongdoing at the state's only public university dedicated to the health care professions, the University of Medicine and Dentistry of New Jersey (UMDNJ). Soon the *New York Times* (2006) would call UMDNJ a "school for scandal." The *Times* wrote that UMDNJ earned this label because, in the eyes of power brokers, it was "a gigantic playground where money can be thrown around with no accountability" while, to legal authorities, "it is a repository of cronyism, corruption and even criminality." Initial charges that UMDNJ's hospitals had double-billed Medicare and Medicaid resulted in the dubious distinction that made UMDNJ "the first medical school in the nation to go under federal supervision" (Ingle and McClure 2009: 10).

As more information became open to public view, I was convinced that UMDNJ was my entry point for the study of corruption. Here was an institution of higher education, relied on by the public to be an authoritative and dependable agent for training and accrediting practitioners who would then go on to make life and death decisions, displaying serious signs of corruption. In the context of higher education, why is corruption the best way to conceptualize such misconduct? How did UMDNJ come to betray, as well as fulfill, its obligations and how could its actions be explained? Was UMDNJ merely an aberration or were its experiences shared with others educating health care professionals? Finding answers to these questions is the rationale for this book.

Why I attach corruption to the events and behaviors that led to investigations at UMDNJ, and found as well at other universities, will be answered in the following section. Other questions require the remainder of the book to answer. Following the discussion of corruption, I begin with an overview of how others have explained why UMDNJ became corrupted. An evaluation of their arguments leads to my own approach, emphasizing organizational responses to environmental changes, and is foreshadowed in this chapter's outline of the book.

Justifying a Label

In using corruption as a concept to subsume UMDNJ's practices, I draw support from a varied literature but one that has not produced a single, agreed-upon definition (Johnston 1996: 321–326). Rather than being an impediment to theoretical clarity, variant definitions, shaped by the disciplinary perspectives of definers (e.g., Dobel 1978: 960; Nye 1967: 419; Werlin 1994; Rose-Ackerman 1999: 9; della Porta and Vannucci 1999), provide guidelines for understanding the broader significance of UMDNJ's behavior by capturing the multi-dimensional meaning of corruption.

Corruption always has a political dimension because its emergence is dependent on inequalities in power. This does not confine it to government officeholders or agencies and their dealings with the public but appears whenever there is "abuse of entrusted power" (Transparency International 2006: xvii; Granovetter 2007: 153). It means that even private actors, like medical personnel or educators who play public roles, are engaged in political relations. Inequalities in power relations are used, often covertly, to provide benefits that exceed the limits that others, particularly those affected by them, consider commensurate with a given position or activities. That is, misuses of power call legitimacy into question. Werlin (1994) conceptualizes how legitimacy may be compromised by locating corruption in the tension between what he calls partisanship – different values underlying struggles over power – and statesmanship – rules of the game for conducting power struggles. Statesmanship imposes limits on how far advantages in power differences can be pursued and corruption occurs where those limits are disregarded. Applied to UMDNJ, this political dimension appears whenever authority was abused to obtain unwarranted power and control.

Those who emphasizes corruption's economic dimension approach it as a principal-agent issue.

> All states, whether benevolent or repressive, control the distribution of valuable benefits and distribution of onerous costs. The distribution of those benefits and costs is generally under the control of public officials who possess discretionary power. Private individuals and firms who want favorable treatment may be willing to pay to obtain it. Payments are corrupt if they are illegally made to public agents with the goals of obtaining a benefit and avoiding a cost.
>
> ROSE-ACKERMAN 1999: 9

The economic perspective sees the world filled with market-like relations, where costs and benefits are weighed, interests compete, and the successful are those who can pay the price for advantage. This economic perspective, when applied to UMDNJ, includes illegal financial activities through which added or excessive resources were sought for either individuals or components of the organization.

Corruption also has a moral dimension (Granovetter 2007: 154; Dobel 1978: 960), manifested in the ethical failures of those in positions of authority. At UMDNJ, examples that challenged the moral boundaries of the health care community involved conflicts of interest and inequitable treatment of faculty, students, or other personnel.

Disaggregating corruption into its three domains – economic, political, and moral – is intended to define its complexity, not to suggest different types of corruption. In practice, all three are interrelated although dimensions can vary in prominence. Moreover, specific actions labeled corrupt may also differ in nature. Some actions are technically illegal. These may involve bribery or its solicitation, extortion, theft, fraud, embezzlement, or conspiracy to commit any of these. Yet not everything that looks like corruption involves breaking the law and not all legal transgressions involving political actors are instances of corruption.[1]

All social relations depend, to some extent, on trust, that is, on confidence that parties to the relationship will behave in expected ways. Violations of trust

1 For some insights see Block's (1996) discussion of the site selection and building of a courthouse in Boston.

are then intrinsic to most definitions of corruption, whether violations involve secret deals, misappropriation of public funds, soliciting or accepting bribes, or using public office for personal advantage. For trustworthy relations to exist there need to be shared norms and values that buttress confidence that all parties in a relationship are following the rules of the game and making decisions in a fair manner. Trustworthiness has special resonance in arenas where wellbeing and even life itself is dependent on services performed by those qualified through their superior skills and information, most acutely so in the case of physicians (Hall et al. 2001). By extension, the training of health practitioners is premised on confidence that applicants begin with the competence to benefit from their education and are then adequately supervised so that they can practice their skills independently. The expectation is that standards will be applied fairly, on the basis of merit. Conflicts of interest, particularly where they involve health care professionals, undermine trust by raising questions about the value of services provided (Robertson et al. 2012: 452).

Another way of conceiving of corruption is as a violation of expectations about the fairness with which power is exerted and rewards distributed. Fairness can be judged in basically two ways. In the first, fairness is presumed to be present when everyone is treated or rewarded equally. Inequality then may be taken as a sign of corruption on the part of those responsible for its occurrence. In the second, although treatment or rewards are unequal, they may still be considered fair because of tradition or merit. Tradition is invoked where special treatment or rewards go to those with ascribed statuses while merit recognizes differences in skills, talents and subsequent achievements as the rationale for inequality. Fairness of this latter kind is a form of distributive justice. Examples of unfair practices include preferential provision of contracts, employment, promotion, or appointments, either to relatives (nepotism) or friends (cronyism), or the direction of rewards to specific constituents (pork barrel politics). The use of patronage in employment or appointments is most overt in emphasizing reciprocal relationships, where rewards are part of an ongoing connection between patrons and those they assist. All these actions may be technically legal while still raising questions about their legitimacy. Such unfair acts are more likely to be questioned where normative expectations are for treatment or rewards to be based on merit, including need.

Moving beyond individual corrupt acts to those that are cumulative, pervasive, and experienced collectively, we enter the level of social organization, where the context may range from a single organization to an entire society. Such corruption has been described with different terminological emphases. Klitgaard (2000), for example, speaks of systemic corruption, where institutions and standards of performance have been undermined.

Lessig (2010) focuses on institutional corruption, which he places within a reciprocal market where influence is used in ways that undermine the effectiveness of an institution and lead to weakened public trust. This emphasis on trust directs attention to the behavior of participants who stray from "legitimate procedures of the institution" (Thompson 2013: 9). It is those institutionalized procedures that otherwise allow an organization to carry out, in predictable and effective ways, activities that are the rationale for its existence. In the case of medical institutions, Thompson (2013: 5) stipulates that such activities "include conducting trustworthy research, providing effective patient care and protecting the public health," to which we can add, for educational institutions, the production of competent professionals. Light (2013), in broadening and clarifying the concept of institutional corruption, emphasizes how it deviates from some acknowledged baseline of integrity. Like Stephenson (2014), and unlike Lessig, he gives space for illegal acts and includes the uses of influence as well as money in producing corruption. When corruption affects the operation of a collective enterprise, nominally good people can be caught up in bad actions.

Among sociologists and business analysts, who focus on how organizations function, a still different terminology is common. Vaughan (1996), for example, speaks of organizational deviance and proposes a theory of how "the normalization of deviance" can come to characterize an organization. Greve et al. (2010: 54) refer to organizational misconduct, which they define as

> behavior in or by an organization that a social-control agent judges to transgress a line separating right from wrong, where such a line can separate legal, ethical, and socially responsible behavior from their antitheses. We define a social-control agent, in turn, as an actor that represents a collectivity and that can impose sanctions on the collectivity's behalf.

This perspective on organizational misconduct, whether internal to an organization or characterizing its relations with others, can be presented as part of its normal operations, the result of the bounded rationality of organizational actors, the influence of the immediate environment, and the cumulative effect of past actions (Palmer 2013). Although I too use deviance and misconduct as ways of characterizing the behavior of UMDNJ or other universities whenever it is appropriate, I do not see those concepts as identical with systemic or institutional corruption. What the former tend to miss is how institutions within the public sector, defined to include higher education, rest on integrity to sustain their legitimacy. Loss of integrity is therefore at the core of corruption.

The multidimensional nature of corruption, the multiple forms in which it is displayed, and the ways corruption exists as an organizational phenomenon all contribute to capturing the nature of UMDNJ's behavior. Those characteristics justify treating UMDNJ as a case of systemic corruption even as it performed its normal functions. They further justify applying the concept of corruption to similar conditions in higher education generally.

Existing Explanations of Corruption

Three commonsense explanations already exist to account for UMDNJ's behavior, focusing on the role of individuals, culture, or organization. While all are plausible, they are limited for the very reason that they focus exclusively on UMDNJ.

Bad Apples

Over the course of reporting on the condition of UMDNJ, the federal monitor emphasized that most employees of UMDNJ had carried out their work conscientiously and honestly (Stern 2006b: 1). In his final report, he reiterated that,

> Our findings over the past two years speak to the moral, ethical, and leadership short-comings of a very few at UMDNJ. Unfortunately, those about whom we were forced to report due to various lapses in judgment often were in decision-making positions.... For every self-serving individual that UMDNJ had had the misfortune to employ, there are hundreds of selfless professionals, physicians, nurses, and professors that UMDNJ should consider itself fortunate to employ.
>
> STERN 2008: 3

The destructive effects of bad apples make them the most visible source for explaining bad outcomes (Sutton 2011). But pointing the finger at bad apples does little to explain the incidence or scale of wrongdoing or even the kinds of individuals who were involved (Palmer 2013: 95–96). Research by social psychologists, even on extreme behavior, concludes that

> many evil actions are not the volitional products of individual evildoers but rather essentially organizational products that result when complex social forces interact to cause individuals to commit multiple acts of terrible harm.
>
> DARLEY 1996: 13–14

Instead of relying on individual characteristics and predispositions to predict when bad behavior occurs, we must look to the organizational context where it takes place. It is there that employees, most of whom see themselves as good people, are led to take part in unethical acts. As Dunn and Schweitzer (2005) point out, to understand the link between the misdeeds of individual actors and the organizations in which they operate requires evaluating the impact of reward systems, organizational culture, and managerial oversight.

The preceding conclusion appears in line with the inclination among sociological organizational theorists to approach agency theory cautiously, if not entirely negatively (e.g., Perrow 1986). Yet the total removal of individual actors from scenarios of corruption would leave many to feel there was something missing. Burt (2012) offers an approach that embeds the agency of individual roles within social networks, suggesting an avenue for more systematically explaining the contribution of individuals to an organization's corruption. But, for the most part, attributing corruption to bad apples is not a productive source of explanation either for UMDNJ or for similar institutions.

Culture

Journalists Bob Ingle and Sandy McClure (2009) used UMDNJ's experiences as the lead-in to their best-selling account of pervasive corruption in New Jersey, which they attribute to a deep-rooted culture that promotes and protects corrupt practices. Their argument rests on two assumptions. The first is that New Jersey is the most corrupt state in the union. The second finds corrupt practices so much a part of the communal life of New Jersey, permeating relations between those in authority and those they are expected to serve, that the state itself has developed a culture that makes it accepted, if not inevitable, that even new relationships will follow a deviant path.

Is New Jersey the most corrupt? The Corporate Crime Reporter (2004) ranked states based on federal prosecutions of public officials at all levels of government from 1993 to 2002. By those measures, the ten most corrupt states began with Mississippi and included, in descending order, North Dakota, Louisiana, Alaska, Illinois, Montana, South Dakota, and Kentucky. Others using the same federal data include Glaeser and Saks (2004) and Dincer and Gunalp (2005). Similar data from 1977 to 1987 form the basis of analyses by Meier and Holbrook (1992) and Hill (2003) while reliance on earlier data is found in Nice (1983) and Johnson (1983). In none of these analyses does New Jersey come out as the worst offender. The most recent review, covering years from 1976 to 2010, ranked New Jersey ninth on the basis of convictions per year and seventh on the basis of convictions per capita (Simpson et al. 2012).

Whether or not such measures give an accurate picture of comparative corruption (Riccards 2012a), not everything that looks like corruption involves breaking the law and not all legal transgressions involving political actors are instances of corruption. These ambiguities affect public views about the meaning and extent of corruption. For example, although there appeared to be widespread concern with corruption during the 2005 New Jersey gubernatorial race, there was no clear consensus about what corruption entailed or who represented the best hopes for limiting it. "[P]olls and interviews show that the meaning of corruption is deeply personal and multitextured – a kind of Rorschach test of the political mind, and because of that, neither candidate, on this topic, has gained a decisive edge" (Gettleman 2005).

Such public uncertainty is one indication that the equation of corruption with culture is too imprecise. The day to day life of New Jersey goes on with most individuals abiding by the law and most organizations following broadly-accepted practices, suggesting that there must be more than one kind of culture in the state. Although there is a respected literature, beginning with Elazar (1972), that classifies states according to their political cultures, Meier and Holbrook (1992) demonstrate that the Elazarian concept of political culture turns out to be a poor predictor of corruption.

Even if New Jersey is not the most corrupt state, any explanation of UMDNJ's actions must take into account the environment New Jersey provided for its operations and the governmental institutions with which it interacted. At least two interacting characteristics are of special note. The first is a lengthy and enduring tradition of contention between two opposing trends, one representing a progressive movement upholding good government and the other, a deeply entrenched machine politics[2] (Salmore and Salmore 2008: 27–52). It is these traditions that underlie opposing political cultures. The second characteristic is the existence of 566 municipalities. "Forty-sixth in size among the states, New Jersey ranks eleventh in total number of municipalities. Their average size is the smallest of any state; one in three is less than two square miles in area" (Salmore and Salmore 2008: 239–261). Those municipalities are entrenched in the governance of the state, ensuring the dominance of local interests and providing multiple opportunities for corrupt behavior. In general, then, explanations of corruption must incorporate the effects of the environment in which higher education is embedded.

Even though Ingle and McClure's concept of a culture of corruption is too broad to demonstrate causality, culture remains relevant to the search for

2 In speaking of this as the tension between "the statesman and the boss," Salmore and Salmore (2008: 381) give credit for this characterization to Rapport (1961).

explanations because all enduring groups develop cultures – ways of perceiving the world and associated repertoires of action. In every complex social organization there will be co-existing multiple cultures that affect and are affected by the institutions they interpenetrate and the organizations that are associated with them (Scott and Davis 2007; Lehman 2006: 24). Individuals, in turn, are carriers of multiple cultures. For example, physicians may simultaneously embody the values and attitudes they absorbed as students and residents, as current faculty members and hospital employees, and as members of professional associations. Although the values derived from each of these settings may reinforce each other, some may give rise to conflicts, leading to uncertainty as to which will prevail. It is this, more complex, conception of culture that helps explain corruption (Palmer 2013: 66–85).

Organizational Structure

The number, range, and persistence of illegal and unethical practices, described in the following chapter, and the unprecedented sanction UMDNJ received through the imposition of a federal monitor make it stand out among its peers. Some of those practices are surely attributable to the unique history of UMDNJ's origins and the organizational makeup that followed. At the same time, when looking at specific instances of misconduct, we find that each had precedent at other universities. Those findings suggest that commonalities in organization must play a role, moderating the effects of any uniqueness.

Since the Office of Inspector General of Health and Human Services began auditing university teaching hospitals in 1995, it has uncovered numerous violations involving overbilling of Medicare and Medicaid and upbilling to more expensive procedures. The principal way overbilling occurs is when the supervising physician is not present and his or her duties are performed by residents or interns, whose services are considered already paid for by government grants for their training. A sampling of those investigated and required to pay substantial fines include the University of Chicago (Leatherman 1999), Georgetown University (Gamble 2012), the University of Washington (Miletich 2005), and the Universities of Pennsylvania, Pittsburgh, and Virginia (Sparrow 2000: 18). The University of California-Irvine Medical School, in addition to having improperly billed Medicare, allowed uncertified personnel to perform procedures, permitted lax oversight over treatments, and fired those who criticized administrative actions (*Los Angeles Times* 1999; Heisel 2005; Fisher 2006). When George Washington's School of Medicine and Health Sciences was put on probation in 2008 on grounds of inadequate supervision of students, further investigation also indicated the potential for serious conflicts of interest

(Kinzie 2009). The chief executive of the Kansas City University of Medicine and Biosciences was accused of misusing university funds for personal benefit while its board of trustees was blamed for lax supervision (Stafford 2010). Harvard medical students created a stir with their charges of undue influence on faculty from pharmaceutical companies and their concern with the consequences this had for what is taught (Wilson 2009).

Other universities' practices, though not confined to their medical schools, provide further instances of misconduct. Those with strong athletic teams can find ways to ensure that players are kept in good standing by persuading faculty to be more lenient toward them or even change their grades (e.g., Sander 2010). Because of pressure to increase national ratings through evidence that only the most qualified students are admitted, universities have responded by either exaggerating SAT scores (Pérez-Peña and Slotnick 2012) or excluding poor scores[3] (Alex 2012a).

Although the extent of undue political intervention into UMDNJ appears to have been unusually high, it is echoed in two examples from the University of Illinois, where I was a faculty member on the Chicago campus for over three decades. In the first example, I was interviewing a political officeholder when he took time to answer a telephone call. He informed the caller, apparently in answer to a request, that there would be no trouble in getting his candidate a teaching position at Governors State University. If true, this would have bypassed official procedures used to search for and hire new faculty. More recently, the University of Illinois was investigated for giving preferential treatment to students applying to the Champaign-Urbana campus, depending on their ties to University trustees, politicians, or large donors (Malone et al. 2009).

Similarities in practices among universities training medical personal, regardless of level of corruption, provide evidence for the organizational basis of corruption. Without either condoning UMDNJ's behavior as merely what everyone else was doing or downplaying the significance of the sheer volume of its offences, the existence of comparable examples increases the likelihood that common causal mechanisms affect all large centers of health-related education. As I document in Chapter 3, these stem most generally from the nature of contemporary higher education in the United States, related changes in medical education, and the structural responses these provoke.

3 Rowan University in New Jersey distorted its grade status to give it a higher score than Rutgers-Camden at the time it stood to gain from a proposed takeover of the latter campus (Alex 2012b).

Outline of the Book

Chapter 1 has set up the problem: how did UMDNJ become corrupted and how does it reflect trends in higher education. The concept of corruption was elaborated to justify its appropriateness when applied to educational institutions. Three common explanations for UMDNJ's corruption were introduced and found to be limited when conceived solely to account for UMDNJ's behavior. Their limitations pointed, paradoxically, to how UMDNJ was more than a special case of a large, state-funded university that, while dedicated to training health care personnel, advancing health-related research, and providing health services to the community, also engaged in widespread unethical and illegal behavior. Instead, they could be shown to highlight how UMDNJ was an exemplar of what could go wrong in such specialized higher education.

Chapter 2 fills in factual details about UMDNJ. Its origins are laid out with an emphasis on how they were the basis of enduring internal conflicts. Instances of corrupt actions are then summarized, ranging over financial, political, and ethical misconduct. The stage is set to account for the co-existence of corruption alongside the normative operation of the university. But to do so, it is necessary to present on a larger canvass the incentives and opportunities for corruption in higher education that arise from pressures in its changing environment. It is this broader context, developed in the following chapter, that will clarify how UMDNJ is an exemplar for understanding institutional corruption.

UMDNJ existed within three interacting worlds of the state, including the federal government as well as that of New Jersey, its counties, and municipalities; the U.S. system of higher education; and the institutions of medical education and related health fields. Collectively, these made up the environment in which UMDNJ operated, as they do for all centers of health care-related education, adjusting for differences in local settings. It is this general milieu that is the subject of Chapter 3, with an emphasis on recent large-scale changes. Changes in education and governmental practices created tensions and uncertainties that enhance the likelihood that a school of health care sciences would be prone to deviant behavior leading to systemic corruption. Using insights from organizational analysis, the chapter concludes with a series of hypotheses anticipating when corruption would be likely to appear.

UMDNJ itself was a complex organization made up of many parts – campuses, schools, hospitals and clinics, departments, and administrative units – each with its own history and problems. The degree of coordination among them varied from close to virtually disconnected. UMDNJ's interactions with its environments placed it in competition for resources with other schools and organizations in the state and nationally. In addition, components of the university at times competed with each other. Moreover, they were often differentially affected by pressures from their environments. A description of the organization of UMDNJ and its governance problems is found in Chapter 4. Guided by hypotheses developed in Chapter 3, it concludes with an assessment of how and where its organizational makeup fostered misconduct.

Chapter 5 continues the focus on UMDNJ's organization by enlarging the network of actors with which it interacted and who played an active role in shaping its behavior. Here I include the character of New Jersey government and its agencies along with other levels of government relevant to UMDNJ's operations. Additional regulatory agencies, professional bodies, and community groups that played influential roles are also contained within the larger network. Again, hypotheses developed in Chapter 3 conclude the chapter by assessing how UMDNJ's network had an impact in encouraging corruption.

From its beginnings, UMDNJ was continually changing shape. Initially, change involved the founding of new schools and departments or the incorporation of already existing ones. Later, UMDNJ looked ripe for reorganization through a breakup of its parts. During the time of writing this book, a breakup was achieved through the state's executive action and legislative support. Chapter 6 assesses these changes with respect to how they were tied to concerns about corruption and how effective they may be in restraining future problems.

Chapter 7 concludes by highlighting the contributions of organizational structures and attendant processes in determining how UMDNJ became a model of scandalous behavior. It moves beyond the confines of UMDNJ to consider how corrupting influences have entered higher education both in the United States and globally to deform training in the health care professions. Even after disappearing as a result of state-mandated restructuring and merger with either Rutgers or Rowan Universities in 2013, UMDNJ remains a critical window for understanding when and why university medical centers may be led to debase their highest ideals. The chapter ends with an assessment of the lessons that may be learned from UMDNJ's experiences.

CHAPTER 2

Sickness in the Midst of Health

To understand how UMDNJ, then the sole comprehensive provider of medical education in New Jersey, came to be stigmatized as a "school for scandal" requires opening up its history and organization, its relations with government, and its interactions with the external agencies that sought to influence it. Such a search is intended to uncover the pathways through which UMDNJ became corrupted and explain why those pathways were followed. This chapter is the first of three that will detail the complex nature of UMDNJ's organization and relations with others. Here we begin by reviewing its origins. In this chapter we also deal with another component of UMDNJ's history – a summary of the behaviors that, taken together, justify the label of corruption.

The origins of UMDNJ in the mid 1960s until its disappearance through restructuring in 2013 provide the larger frame for viewing UMDNJ. Within that frame, this analysis concentrates on events beginning in the mid 1990s, when evidence of wrongdoing raised a new uneasiness about the administration of the University, until the mid 2000s, when the federal monitor appointed to oversee the University's operation and collect data on its problems presented his final report.

Origins of UMDNJ

UMDNJ had twofold origins as a state university, both surrounded by enduring controversy. One beginning occurred when Seton Hall, a private Catholic college, received a charter to establish a College of Medicine and Dentistry in 1954 in Jersey City. When that college soon ran into financial and administrative problems, Seton Hall tried to persuade Rutgers University to take it over but Rutgers refused the offer. Seton Hall, however, had strong political connections, made evident when Governor Richard J. Hughes appointed a committee to determine the medical school's fate. The committee was headed by George F. Smith, former president of Johnson and Johnson, and made up of two former governors, the president of Merck Pharmaceuticals, the presidents of the state medical and dental societies and the NJ Taxpayers Association. After reviewing the college's assets, the committee recommended that it be purchased by the state. It was duly acquired in 1965, named the New Jersey College of Medicine and Dentistry and renamed the College of Medicine and Dentistry of New Jersey (CMDNJ) in 1970. The state began plans to relocate CMDNJ to Newark, a move that acquired new impetus with the 1967 riots in that city (Mumford 2007). The first move occurred in 1968 and expansion continued through the next decade.

The second origin was indigenous to the state system of higher education. Its prelude began in 1961, when Rutgers University established Rutgers Medical School (RMS), which began with the first two years of medical education. It hired Dr DeWitt Stetten, Jr, a respected biochemist, as dean, with the goal of developing a strong research-oriented medical school. Through his professional contacts, Stetten was made aware that the American Association of Medical Colleges was raising questions about the quality of Seton Hall's program (Stetten 1983). He was then instrumental in having Rutgers reject the takeover of the Seton Hall school. But there were new political developments in the state, beginning with the creation of a Chancellor of Higher Education and the subsequent plan to separate RMS from its University. That plan was approved by the legislature in 1970, when RMS became part of the CMDNJ. It would have a full medical curriculum while keeping its separate identity and be renamed Robert Wood Johnson Medical School (RWJMS).[1]

University status was awarded by the legislature in 1981 and the College was renamed the University of Medicine and Dentistry of New Jersey (UMDNJ). Each medical school remained distinct, with its own physical location, administration, faculty, and teaching hospitals. Students seeking admission did so by applying to the specific school of choice.

Continued growth made UMDNJ the largest freestanding school of health sciences in the United States, with eight schools on five campuses. New Jersey Medical School (NJMS) and the School of Dentistry were located in Newark; Robert Wood Johnson had campuses in New Brunswick, Piscataway, and Camden. The Graduate School of Biomedical Sciences, a separate entity since 1969, had campuses in Newark, Stratford and Piscataway. The School of Osteopathic Medicine (SOM), located in Stratford and Camden, was founded in 1976, initially relying on RWJMS in Piscataway for the first two years of the basic science curriculum. The School of Health Related Professions, begun in 1977, had sites in Stratford, Newark, and Piscataway and, in 1998, received official status for its campus in Scotch Plains, specifically designed to serve non-traditional, part-time students (Orlando 1998). The School of Nursing, founded

---

1 But Stetten (1983) would not be part of the change, resigning from his position and blaming the Rutgers Board for not defending the University's interests and the Association of American Medical Colleges for not being forthcoming about the situation at Seton Hall.

in 1992, had locations in Newark and Stratford. The School of Public Health was a joint venture of UMDNJ, Rutgers University, and the NJ Institute of Technology. One campus was established in 1983 in Piscataway/New Brunswick; another, begun in 1999, in Newark; and a third, begun in 2001, in Stratford/Camden.

The education and training of UMDNJ's approximately 6000 students and the advancement of medical knowledge took place in classrooms, scientific laboratories, and clinical settings. Twenty-four research centers were either directly a part of the University or affiliated with it. Primary teaching hospitals were University Hospital in Newark, affiliated with NJMS; Robert Wood Johnson University Hospital in New Brunswick and Cooper University Hospital in Camden, affiliated with RWJMS; and Kennedy Health System/University Medical Center, with locations in Stratford, Cherry Hill, and Washington Townships, affiliated with SOM. Only University Hospital was fully owned by UMDNJ; the other primary teaching hospitals were affiliated through contractual relations. The University had additional affiliations with major teaching hospitals and clinical practices in 14 counties, supplemented by health care facilities and a behavioral health care network in six counties. Looser educational and clinical affiliations extended throughout the state and involved about 300 facilities. All affiliations were exclusively either with NJMS, RWJMS, or SOM.

Responsibility for this immense enterprise fell under the purview of the state and federal governments and external accrediting agencies. The University followed state regulations in such matters as hiring, contracts, and safety measures, in return for which it received funding for its operations. It was overseen by a Board of Trustees appointed by the Governor with input from legislative leaders. The President, the most visible figure representing the University, was ostensibly hired by the trustees but, in practice, the Governor was usually the major agent in making the appointment. The federal government was a critical partner, as it is with all academic medical centers, through its regulation of research and training and its provision of funding for research and medical care. The University as a whole, along with its component departments and affiliated hospitals, were subject to review by multiple accrediting agencies. Those agencies look for evidence of competent administration, evaluated, in the case of students, through high proportions able to pass licensing exams and, in the case of patients, high proportions successfully receiving appropriate treatment. In addition, the University contracted with a number of professional associations and unions over salaries and working conditions.

By virtue of its size, geographic dispersion, and the importance of its educational and public health mandates, the UMDNJ was not only a major enterprise in the state but one enjoying the added prestige associated with health care professionals, particularly physicians.[2] Moreover, the life-enhancing possibilities that come from healing the sick give the practice of medicine, including the training of practitioners, an unquestioned moral authority[3] that allows viewing a medical center as a community bound by standards of behavior emphasizing fairness and integrity. Yet none of these attributes could protect UMDNJ from accusations of serious malfeasance, brought to a head in 2005 by the intervention of federal authorities.

UMDNJ Corrupted

Chapter 1 presented corruption as a multidimensional concept with multiple forms of expression. That conceptualization offers an economical way to classify the different kinds of misdeeds that were found at UMDNJ.

Financial Misconduct

Charges brought against UMDNJ with the most serious implications were financial ones, tied to improper billing of Medicare and Medicaid and at the heart of the complex relations linking medical centers with their teaching hospitals. Compared to other hospitals, university-affiliated ones are more likely to provide innovative (and hence expensive) care, often to patients that come to them precisely because of their complex disorders. Moreover, they may be located in areas that serve large numbers of uninsured patients, as was the case of University Hospital in Newark. Payments for medical services were, next to money provided directly by the state, the most important source of revenues

---

2 Studies of occupational prestige, extrapolated to occupational categories listed in the US census, produced a mean occupational prestige rating of 43.43. Physicians were rated at the top with a score of 86.03 while scientists averaged about 73 (Nakao and Treas 1992). Further study confirms positive evaluations for physicians even though there was a noticeable decline in satisfaction with their performance between 1976 and 1988 (Pescosolido et al. 2001: 7–9). Confidence in these findings is high, given the remarkable stability in how different publics rate occupations across time and societies (Hauser and Warren 1997: 188–190.) The esteem of occupations generally is attributed to their relative authority and the resources they command (Treiman 1977) or to the recognition that comes from legitimacy and appropriateness (Zhou 2005).

3 In surveys between 1973 and 2006, in which Americans were asked about their confidence in 13 institutions, the two with the highest mean scores were medicine and the scientific community. Education, undifferentiated by level, was fifth, closely following the military and the Supreme Court (Smith 2008).

for the University, and their importance holds true for all university medical centers in the United States. But as the environment for such funding has altered, universities have been pressed to reorganize relations with their hospitals, leaving both to operate in a highly uncertain world (Cohen 1998; Schmidt 1996). For some, uncertainty would promote fraud.

When the Office of Inspector General of the U.S. Department of Health and Human Services discovered that Medicare was being billed for physicians' services that were in fact performed by residents[4] and for "upcoding" to more complicated procedures from the less complicated ones actually done, it began a nationwide program in 1995 for auditing university teaching hospitals. When offences are uncovered, they may be turned over to the Justice Department for redress, as they were in the case of UMDNJ in 2005. Once on the scene in NJ, investigators found about one hundred additional instances of wrongdoing (Ingle and McClure 2009: 11) and raised the initial dollar amount in question almost a hundred-fold when other waste and fraud were included (Ingle and McClure 2009: 18). The final report of the Federal Monitor listed over $157 million in cost-reporting errors affecting both the state and federal governments (Stern 2008: 6).

Billing practices at UMDNJ were closely tied to how medical faculty was reimbursed. In addition to a negotiated academic base salary, other salary components were related to patient care. One component derived from treatment of charity cases, calculated without regard to how many patients were involved. That amount tended to remain stable over the years. It also offered some discretionary application, allowing administrators to use the money for activities other than patient care. It helped, for example, to attract new hires with a supplemented salary that exceeded their academic base. The second component came from faculty practice plans – independent non-profit corporations run by faculty members to bill, collect, and distribute clinical receipts based on the contributions of members to patient practice.[5] Income from practice plans, whether to individual members or to their departments, could vary by year, depending on success in collecting fees from patients or their insurers.

Although the Justice Department began its scrutiny of UMDNJ in 2005, overbilling of Medicare and Medicaid had been recognized internally at least since

4 That government department was already paying for the training of residents in teaching hospitals, making it the largest funder of graduate medical education.

5 Each medical school had its own faculty practice plan: University Physician Associates at NJMS, University Medical Group at RWJMS, and the practice plan at the School of Osteopathic Medicine. In addition, nurses and dentists had their own plans.

1993 (Department of Justice 2009). It had its origins in a court ruling from 1983, interpreted to give physicians the right to bill for services. With the university administration insisting that only its affiliated hospitals had the right to bill, the solution had turned into double billing (Santiago 2009). The University's computer system was also configured to charge the maximum possible reimbursement rate. No further details were uncovered about the processes by which these billing procedures became institutionalized or the administrators responsible for them.

Eventually, all the medical faculty practice plans were implicated but initially the focus was on University Physicians Associates (UPA) and its contentious relations with NJMS (Stern 2006a: 43–46). The Board of Trustees had not included UPA's financial statements in reviewing the consolidated statements of the University "since they were deemed not material" (Stern 2006a). University administrators who had tried to draw attention to these suspect practices were forced to leave (Margolin and Sherman 2005a; b) although some were prepared to strike back.[6]

When U.S. Attorney Chris Christie confronted the University's Board of Trustees with evidence of improper billing, he presented them with limited choices. His office would recommend to the U.S. District Court, following the filing of a criminal complaint for health care fraud, that it defer prosecution for up to 36 months. That deferral was contingent on continuing remediation, full restitution of improperly received federal money, and supervision by a federal monitor (Deferred Prosecution Agreement 2005; Margolin and Sherman 2005b). After the Trustees agreed, former judge Herbert J. Stern assumed the role of monitor, ending his mandated term three years later with over 40 files still open for investigation. During the period of supervision, the monitor uncovered additional issues over billing, coding, and inflated reimbursements (Stern 2008).

As a result of overbilling Medicaid, the State of New Jersey's Charity Care program had been affected as well. The federal monitor estimated that, between 2001 and 2005, the state had overpaid UMDNJ by 11.7 million. Further investigation was also prompted by the University's status as a "nominal charge provider," in which it charged less than the cost of care. To compensate for this, the state enacted legislation covering years 1998 to 2000 to give the University an extra appropriation of 51 million. However, its billing policies put UMDNJ's status as a nominal charge provider in doubt and raised the likelihood that, not only would it need to recompensate the state, but that the state itself would be

6 Among the whistleblowers were Adam Henick, a former vice president (Moran 2005), and Dr Steven S. Simring, who collected $801,000 for his revelations (Santiago 2009; Amirault 2009).

liable for the half of the 51 million that had been provided it by the federal government (Stern 2006d: 6–7).

The market in which the University conducted its business was also the setting for a range of other questionable actions. For example, despite both University regulations and state law that cover requisitioning goods and services, no-bid contracts in violation of these were widespread and accounted for over 202 million dollars from 2002 to 2006 (Stern 2008). Documents released by the University for one fiscal year, covering 2003–04, indicated that more than 170 million dollars in no-bid contracts were awarded, of which more than 140 million dollars were approved by the Trustees without them knowing the names of the vendors (Margolin and Heyboer 2005a).

Once the federal monitor had begun his investigations, the President and Board of Trustees undertook their own effort to collect data on questionable practices related to procurements, particularly of contracts where bids had been waived. Garry S. Stein, an attorney with the New Jersey firm of Pashman Stein, and assisted by the accounting firm of Morrison and Company, reviewed all contracts issued in fiscal year 2005, with special attention to 240 contracts valued at under 50 million dollars. Of those, 102, valued at under 17 million dollars, were found to have been incorrectly approved. Stein (2006: 5–6) faulted the University's Purchasing Department and Office of Legal Management for permitting such a large number of waivers, calling their behavior "inexcusable," reflecting "a careless and undisciplined approach to the correct application of the public bidding statutes," yet found no evidence of corruption with respect to vendors.

Stein's narrow view of what constituted corruption, however, glosses over the reality that "carelessness" over contracts brought together abuses that involved financial gain and inappropriate uses of power by university personnel. Support for this broader interpretation of corruption comes from the report of the State Commission of Investigation (SCI), called on to investigate higher education by Acting Governor Richard Codey in 2005.[7] SCI provides the example of Circle Janitorial Supplies, Inc. (CJS) to document how contracts were abused, regardless of whether or not they were subject to bidding.

> The Commission found that UMDNJ's contracts with CJS were written in such a way to render the university vulnerable to exorbitant and unwarranted overcharges - sometimes to the tune of more than 100 percent of

7 Although UMDNJ was the catalyst for SCI's (2007) work, its report was based on a broader inquiry into the system of higher education in the state, with special attention reserved for both UMDNJ and Rutgers University.

> the original cost of the item - and that UMDNJ officials have done little or nothing until recently to stem the loss of hundreds of thousands of dollars over the years. The investigation also revealed that CJS's officials had provided gifts and benefits to numerous UMDNJ employees, including [Assistant Vice President Ernestine] Watson, in order to ingratiate themselves.
>
> STATE COMMISSION OF INVESTIGATION 2007: 20–25

Further overlap between the financial and political realms of corrupt behavior was evident as well in the practice of vendors making gifts to UMDNJ employees. One such vendor was Cesario Construction Company Ltd, which had forged a relationship with Francis X. Watts, Jr, a plumber who became acting director of the Physical Plant, and who was responsible for awarding all emergency work to that company. Cesario rewarded Watts by building a deck on the latter's home and paying for its reconstruction (State Commission of Investigation 2007: 25–27).

Political Misconduct

Issues of power and control, while endemic to any complex organization, have even broader implications in the case of a state institution with perilously close relations to the representatives of government that established and supervised it. The geographic dispersion of the University's campuses, its teaching hospitals, and related services opened doors to influence from local politicians. The result was that, alongside the University's reliance on the formal qualifications of employees at all levels, there also existed an informal patronage system tied to state and local politicians, expanded and routinized under President John Petillo.[8] Applicants were ranked from 1 to 3, with 1 given to those who had the most important connections with politicians like U.S. Representative (now Senator) Robert Menendez, then Mayor Sharpe James of Newark, State Senator Robert Lesniak, and then State Senator Wayne Bryant, chairman of the senate budget committee (Stern 2006a: 76–77). Menendez was said to have been unaware that his recommendations, allegedly made in the interests of adding diversity to the university, were given preferential treatment. Lesniak indicated that he had made only one recommendation of a dentist who had to stop practicing because of Parkinson's disease but whom

8 John Petillo, with a doctorate in counseling, had been chancellor of Seton Hall University and chief executive of Blue Cross Blue Shield of New Jersey, when Governor McGreevey first appointed him to the Board of Trustees, where he became chairman. The Governor later named Petillo first interim president and then, in 2004, the official president.

Lesniak thought would be an excellent teacher (Kocieniewski 2006a). It is not known how many people were hired in this fashion but, at the time of investigation, over 25 were in the pool recommended for positions as security guards, secretaries, and researchers. Even though some applicants had already been rejected, human relations personnel reported that they were under strong pressure to respond to Dr Petillo's number one recommendations (Stern 2006a: 77; Kocieniewski 2006b).

Conscious of how dependent they were on state officials for resources and, in some cases, for their positions, some administrators proactively sought to protect their interests. Under the presidency of Dr Stanley S. Bergen, Jr, who held office from 1971 to 1998, Steven Adubato, described as a Newark community leader, was hired as director of external affairs for a two-year period beginning in 1989, paid from the president's discretionary fund. His job was "troubleshooting" with local, county and state governments. Specific issues of concern to the University involved a dispute with the county over payment for inmate health care; with the city, over the cost of ambulance services; and with the state, in finding ways to obtain greater autonomy. Adubato does not appear to have been successful in settling any of them (Whitlow 1991).

Adubato continued to be an influential political force through the loyalties he generated in running a social service network that enabled him to deliver votes from his corner of Newark. Later he would push for the appointment of John Petillo as University President, solidifying the ties between the University and his sector of Newark (Kocieniewski and Sullivan 2006). Those ties would be of direct benefit to him and to his son, Steven Adubato Jr. The elder Adubato ran a medical and social service agency for the elderly, Casa Israel, that he described as alleviating patient use of emergency services at University Hospital. He subsequently proposed that his agency provide further assistance to patients discharged from University Hospital but, in fact, its resources were not adequate for the job. The University responded by embarking on a pilot program with Casa Israel which led to the latter requesting further funding. The Foundation of the University of Medicine and Dentistry Foundation[9] provided President Petillo with a discretionary fund, from which he was able to grant $95,000 to the agency (Stern, 2006: 157–162). The junior Adubato obtained no-bid contracts with the University in 2004 and 2005 to both produce a six-part public television series and a separate series publicizing the Cancer Institute of New Jersey (Stern 2006: 138–142). Adubato Jr, who also had interests

9 The Foundation, originally established in 1974 by a small group of businessmen, is a 501(c)(5) organization based on private contributions and free to support any aspect of UMDNJ's objectives.

in professional development and executive training, was able to sell these services to the University in the form of a series of workshops at three of its campuses. Those contracts were approved by Senior Vice President for Academic Affairs Robert Saporito, who, in connection with the training contract, later admitted that "he inadvertently had authorized the agreement without realizing that public bidding was required" (Stern 2006: 144).

Hiring lobbyists to obtain favorable access to state and federal governments was a growing practice, used by UMDNJ in ways to avoid contract-bidding procedures and thus allow administrators discretion to enhance their own power. Chip Stapleton, a Republican consultant and friend of then Senate President Donald DiFrancesco, was hired in 1995 to recommend ways to "enhance the state recognition and reputation of the university." But in the 10 years he was employed, there was no written record of any work he may have done (Margolin 2005b). When payment of $75,000 from UMDNJ to Robert White, a Philadelphia power broker, came to light in an unrelated corruption trial in his home city, it revealed that White had been hired to keep the University updated on newly-elected Governor McGreevey's policies and plans, which included merging UMDNJ with Rutgers University. Again, no records were found to show that White, who had been one of the Governor's top fund raisers, had done anything for the money (Margolin and McNichol 2005). By this time, McGreevey had resigned and Acting Governor Codey called on the State Commission of Investigation (SCI) to examine this and other abuses. The SCI documented additional information on the discretionary use of lobbyists, including their role in damage control following publicity over the investigations of UMDNJ that were underway (State Commission of Investigation 2007: 54–55).

Direct support for politicians was also part of the University's strategy for ensuring favorable responses from them. While presumably using the president's discretionary fund that was not based on public moneys, UMDNJ gave three contributions, totaling $1800, to Assembly Speaker Garabed (Chuck) Haytaian, a Republican from Warren County, between 1992 and 1993 (Braun 1994). In 2003 the University gave Newark Mayor Sharpe James a donation of $1000 from an account supported from private donations. The mayor, who, at the time, also held a seat in the legislature, had a magnified importance because his city was the locale for NJMS and its affiliated hospital. In 2001, the University donated $4800 to Republican Donald DiFrancesco, who had filled the unfinished term of Governor Whitman and then entered the governor's race (*Star-Ledger* 2003a). Christy Davis Jackson, University Vice President for governmental affairs, authorized donations of $500 to Mayor Sharpe James, $250 to the Democratic State Committee, and $50 to the Hispanic American PAC of Union County, the location of the Scotch Plains campus of the School of Health Related Professions. After being reprimanded for violating University policy, she made reimbursement.

Davis Jackson had only recently been hired by President Petillo from her job as a lobbyist for Babyland Family Services, a Newark nonprofit founded by the mother of Newark Councilwoman Gayle Chaneyfield-Jenkins, and the former's ties with Newarks's community organizations were a source of contention. Davis Jackson had earlier authorized a $10,000 donation to an unregistered charity run by Councilwoman Chaneyfield-Jenkins to promote cancer awareness. With the University now faced with new scrutiny of its financial practices, the Board of Trustees agreed that the donation was an improper use of state funds. The presence at the Board meeting by the Councilwoman and her supporters and support for her position from Trustee Donald Bradley, who was also president of the Newark City Council, became an ocassion for disruptive and racist name-calling (Margolin 2005a).

Most egregious were the University's relations with State Senator Wayne Bryant whose base was the impoverished city of Camden. While chairman of the Senate Budget and Appropriations Committee, Bryant was hired by the University in 2003 as a part-time consultant, although without any specified duties. The job was created for him through the auspices of R. Michael Gallagher, dean of the School of Osteopathic Medicine (SOM) (Stern 2006e). Bryant had earlier been influential in having SOM establish a location in Camden and, over the three years he held his new position, he ensured that state moneys were generously directed to the school. For example, in the course of one year, Bryant was able to double SOM's state funding (Stern 2006e: 2). Later, he helped Dean Gallagher obtain unwarranted incentive bonuses (Ingle and McClure 2009: 10).

Ethical Lapses

Commonly held understandings about how medical education should operate ethically were called into question in multiple ways, implied in many of the preceding examples. One form of unethical behavior was demonstrated by the cardiothoracic training program at NJMS and University Hospital. Although the behavior involved was clearly illegal, I present it here because it represented gross violations of trust between physicians and patients and between faculty and students. The program had been under probation by the Accreditation Council for Graduate Medical Education since 2002. Accreditation was terminated on June 30, 2005 for, among other reasons, a case volume too low to provide adequate training, a deficiency evident for years previously. In addition, since 2002, two of three graduates had failed to achieve board certification. This went along with University Hospital's history of high mortality rates (Stewart 2005a). Among its efforts to improve the situation, beginning in 2002, NJMS hired 18 local cardiologists as salaried clinical assistant professors, each earning up to $150,000, with no responsibilities for teaching or supervision of medical students. Instead, they were expected to refer their patients to University Hospital in order to bolster its surgical program. But under federal law, it is a crime to pay for such kick-backs and the Stark law makes it illegal to profit from the referral of patients (Sherman and Margolin 2006b). Those blamed for devising, aiding, and abetting the scheme included Vice President and Administrator for Finance James Archibald, CEO of University Hospital Sidney Mitchell, head of the Department of Medicine Jerrold Ellner, and Vice President for Legal Management Vivian Sanks King. Even while under federal monitorship, the University compounded its difficulties by paying $2.2 million to settle a whistle-blower suit brought by Dr Rohit Arora, former chief of cardiology, who alleged he was forced to resign because he objected to the hirings (Superior Court of New Jersey 2003; Margolin and Sherman 2006c).

Another area in which unfairness was evident was in administrative discretion over compensation policies. Although the President was required to approve travel expenses for senior vice presidents, they regularly bypassed him as well as other rules on travel. Over five years, beginning in 2000, 31 top administrators recorded over $631,000 in travel, with Vice President for Finance and Administration James Archibald standing out as the single top spender (Margolin and Heyboer 2005b). Although the amount involved was considerably less, Senior Vice President for Academic Affairs Robert Saporito drew the attention of the federal monitor because "Saporito's attitude of entitlement is entirely inappropriate for an individual in his position"(Stern 2006a: 75). In 2004 alone, UMDNJ spent about $3 million in bonuses to administrators and managers. Moreover, it gave senior officials leaving the university an equivalent of a "golden parachute," comprising up to two years of salary, and including, at times, health and pension benefits, cars, free office space and clerical assistance, and other amenities (State Commission of Investigation 2007: 66).

The increasing influence of pharmaceutical companies on medical education and practice is now a major source of concern (Brennan et al. 2006), discussed in the following chapter. Chapters 5 and 6 document the influential role played by past and current executives of the pharmaceutical companies on state-appointed committees affecting the administration of UMDNJ. In addition, the *Star-Ledger* raised questions over the propriety of naming a new children's hospital, part of the RWJUH complex, for Bristol-Meyers Squibb (Editorial 1999). The company was favored in this way because of its pledge of five million dollars to the hospital.

At the Camden campus of RWJMS, the Senior Associate Dean for Academic and Student Affairs, Paul Mehne, pressed faculty to give passing grades to students who had failed to complete required clerkships. In support of allegations against Mehne, the monitor considered it suspicious that, over a six year period, few if any students on the Camden campus, unlike those on the New Brunswick campus, were referred to the Academic Standing Committee over grade issues (Stern 2007: 4). In addition, the monitor determined other improprieties related to students, including financial dealings and unwarranted removal of records (Stern 2007; Johnson 2007).

Violations of trust with respect to the fair and equitable treatment of students were also present in the School of Osteopathic Medicine. Warren Wallace, while working under Dean Gallagher as the self-described second ranking official at the school, attempted to ensure the admission of his own daughter to SOM even though she did not submit results from the Medical College Aptitude Test, letters of recommendation, or the required essays. He was also alleged to have tried to get a no-bid contract for a friend's cafeteria and catering services (Stern 2006c). Wallace, also a freeholder in Gloucester County, adjacent to Camden County, had close ties to Senator Bryant and had used his political connections to help Gallagher become dean (Moroz 2007). The federal monitor considered the amount of time Wallace spent on his political activities to be inappropriate for his university role.

The School of Osteopathic Medicine was encumbered by actions of its dean, Michael Gallagher, who was accused of financial fraud, cronyism, and double dipping (Stern 2006b: 3–18). Gallagher was also the subject of charges brought by Dr George E. Piper, who had been Associate Dean for Graduate Medical Education (GME), a position he had held since 1994. Piper alleged in a law suit that,

> At several meetings of the Executive Council Meeting between April and June 2004, plaintiff was asked to change certain statistics UMDNJ-SOM reported to *U.S. News and World Report* magazine to reflect a higher percentage of the UMDNJ-SOM graduates going into primary care medicine. Plaintiff was asked to count traditional rotating interns as entering primary care medicine although, according to plaintiff, those students generally entered speciality residencies. Plaintiff objected and indicated that he believed changing the statistics would be fraudulent.
>
> SUPERIOR COURT OF NEW JERSEY 2011: 3

Subsequently, Dean Gallagher appointed a task force to consider the future direction of GME that heard a complaint from a staff member which appeared to implicate Piper in a punitive performance evaluation. Within months, the Dean removed Piper as Associate Dean and the latter returned to his department at a lower base salary. After further internal investigation that failed to support Piper, he resigned from the University in 2006 and, several months later, filed a complaint under the Conscientious Employee Protection Act. His original claim was dismissed, as was his appeal, on grounds that it was not filed within the statutory time limits (Superior Court of New Jersey 2011). Meanwhile, the precipitating event, relating to the manipulation of statistics in order to cast SOM in a more favorable light, was never addressed.

The School of Dentistry was troubled by an atmosphere of lax supervision of students. In 2006, twenty dental students were denied diplomas because of systematic cheating. Some had been given credit for course work they had not done; others had developed a scheme for sharing information about examination questions (Ingle and McClure 2009: 15; Sherman and Margolin 2006a). In less than one year, a second cheating scandal was revealed (Sherman and Margolin 2007).

All these examples involving students are recognized as threats to academic integrity in a global context (Heyneman 2013: 103). Failure to curtail student misconduct can undermine a university's reputation and devalue the worth of its degrees. As a result, they belong in an assessment of corruption because of their effect on core values of fairness and trust.

Trustworthiness was compromised as well by multiple instances of conflict of interest among the University's Trustees, appointed by the Governor and approved by the legislature to serve five-year terms. The essentially partisan nature of their appointments was never disguised any more than were their personal ties to politicians. For example, when Governor Whitman nominated Dr Arnold Derman, a radiologist and husband of a state judge who was her former chief of staff, it aroused complaint from Senator Richard Codey, an influential Democrat whose district encompassed Essex County. He accused the Governor of using patronage – hardly shocking in this context – and pointed out that only one trustee came from Essex County, the site of a large part of the university's operations (Scott 1998a). Similarly, State Senator Anthony Bucco tried to block the appointment of Lester Lieberman to replace Stephen Weinstein as trustee. The latter two were Democrats and, although Senator Bucco was a Republican, he alleged that his opposition had the backing of Democratic State Senator Ronald Rice as well as that of the Morris County Democratic chairman. (Morris County is adjacent to both Essex and Union counties.) Weinstein was also Senator Bucco's personal attorney (Ragonese 2003).

Trustee appointments by Governor McGreevey appear to have generated greatest concern over conflicts of interest. Harvey Holzberg, who was initially appointed by the Governor as chairman, was simultaneously president of the Robert Wood Johnson University Hospital in New Brunswick. He resigned from the Board in 2003, pressed by faculty over his dual roles (Stewart 2005b). Pressure for his removal came from local politicians, concerned that Holzberg's loyalties were to New Brunswick rather than Newark, the site of the University's central administration and of University Hospital. With Holzberg in mind, State Senators Sharpe James (also mayor of Newark) and Ronald Rice, Democrats from Essex County, and Anthony Bucco, Republican from Morris County, introduced a bill prohibiting any official of a hospital affiliated with UMDNJ from serving on the Board of Trustees (Stewart and Lane 2002). Former President Bergen joined with Steve Adubato, executive director of the North Ward Center in Newark, a local Essex County party boss formerly employed by Dr Bergen as a government affairs expert, to ensure that Holzberg leave the Board (Patterson 2004). Adubato complained of Holzberg's close ties with John A. Lynch Jr, a local power broker in Middlesex County (Kocieniewski and Sullivan 2006). But overlapping affiliations between the UMDNJ board and that of Robert Wood Johnson University Hospital still continued, involving trustees Christopher Paladino, Eric S. Pennington, John Hoffman, and John Petillo prior to the latter becoming UMDNJ President.

In addition, trustees of this period had many questionable connections with business and politics. During his tenure as a trustee, John Petillo headed the Newark Alliance, a business group concerned with that city's economic revitalization. Christopher Paladino was a developer who had done work for UMDNJ, including building campus housing in Newark. The interim Board chair became Sonia Delgado, a health care lobbyist whose company's clients included the Robert Wood Johnson University Hospital. John Hoffman was a managing partner in a law firm that worked on a campus housing project. Additionally, John Ferguson served on the board while president and CEO of Hackensack University Medical Center, a hospital affiliated with the New Jersey Medical School. Newark City Council President Donald Bradley was a trustee whose city had contracts with UMDNJ. Bradley's own appointment to the Board was tied to pressure to increase the representation of minorities (Stewart 2003a). He was alleged to have pushed the University to employ his friends and relatives and to have negotiated a dollar a year rental of UMDNJ space for a campaign donor (Stern, 2006b: 19–35; Margolin and Heyboer 2006).

On Governor McGreevey's resignation, Senate leader Richard Codey became Acting Governor and moved to put his own stamp on the board. The board had already defied him by refusing to cut millions in bonuses for university administrators. Governor Codey allied himself with Trustee Sonia Delgado, who favored bonus cuts as part of a reform agenda that would reconsider such perks as luxury cars and chauffeurs. Delgado had been an aide to Codey and was already in a struggle with President Petillo (Margolin 2005c). One nominee for an open position on the board was Anthony B. Terracciano, a former bank executive already connected to the state as a member of the State Investment Council, a group that sets policy for the state's investment portfolio. He came with the recommendation of Senator Raymond Lesniak, an influential politician from Union County. Senator Lesniak also recommended the second nominee, Dr Victor Daibo, an orthopedic surgeon who lived in his county (Sherman 2005).[10] Especially relevant were the Senator's ties to Newark Mayor Sharpe James (later convicted of unrelated abuses), whom he represented on the citizens' committee that participated in the search for the UMDNJ president that selected John Petillo. Senator Lesniak also received substantial workers' compensation referrals from the city, a source of conflict because of the contracts between the city and University Hospital (Sherman 2005).

During the period in question, the Board of Trustees disregarded any expectations that their roles required them to uphold the trust of both the University community and the taxpayers of New Jersey. Members used their connections with the University to further their own interests and those of their friends and families. For example, the federal monitor charged that the secretary of the board, Dr Frederic C. Sterritt, had improperly used his position to obtain employment at the University for a relative (Stern 2006d: 42–44; Kocieniewski 2006a). Even when trustees did not actively place their interests above the University's, they still did not take seriously their job as overseers, demonstrated by their laxity over no-bid contracts (Boozang 2007–2008: 96).

Concerns about violations of trust also arose from the agreement signed by the Board of Trustees in December 2005, in which they agreed that the University would abide by the conditions set by US Attorney Christie to avoid prosecution (Deferred Prosecution Agreement 2005). Among items agreed on was the provision of all documents that the federal monitor would request. In one sense, the agreement was after the fact, since the FBI and the US Attorney's Office had already begun subpoenaing documents in June 2005, almost six months before the trustees gave their signature. But what followed raised suspicions when the first of what would become many break-ins into

---

10 Dr Daibo, who withdrew from consideration, was found to have been involved in disputes in two hospitals where he had privileges.

University administrative offices began at the end of July. Entry to the building was made with a university card and theft was primarily of financial files (Margolin and Heyboer 2005c). Break-ins continued in the same offices even though a new entry system meant that the thief could no longer use the same card and had to rely on a crow bar. Administrators denied that any of the subpoenaed documents had been taken but suspicion remained high. According to Alexander Menza, a member of the Board of Trustees and a retired Superior Court judge, "Some of the stuff that's taken is so petty, so minuscule it doesn't make sense." But he felt that could be a ruse. "Those things are done all the time. People would commit a major crime and take a tin of pennies to indicate it was something else" (Margolin and Heyboer 2005d).

An Unhealthy Example

From this overview of events and practices found at UMDNJ, "school for scandal" seems a perfectly justified label. The University's financial integrity was blemished and its relations with students, patients, and state taxpayers compromised. The result was a case of systemic corruption.

UMDNJ's origins from two competing medical schools, its geographic dispersion, and its sheer size and complexity give some hints to how it became corrupted. More definitive information on the links between UMDNJ's structures and relationships will be revealed in future chapters where we examine how UMDNJ was organized internally and in relation to its environment. But in order to make that examination effective, UMDNJ needs to be moved out of its singular status into the world of higher education generally. The changes and tensions in that world, explored in the following chapter, provide the context in which UMDNJ's problems arose and the guidelines for explaining its path to corruption.

CHAPTER 3

Educational Conditions and Environments

The position taken to this point is that corruption of the kind displayed by UMDNJ has its roots in how organizations respond to pressures, whether generated from their own histories or from interactions with their changing environments. This chapter provides an overview of how pressures emerge and how they shape corrupt responses. In other words, here is the general argument to account for the corruption of higher education, as applicable to UMDNJ as it is other universities in a similar situation.

Universities in the United States[1] operate in a complex and uncertain world where virtually everything they do may be subject to dispute, whether by their own administrators, faculty, students, politicians, governmental and non-governmental regulators, business, the mass media, neighbors, or special interests. Understanding the resulting pressures on higher education and how they have evolved in recent years is the initial goal of this chapter. The condition of higher education is then the context for describing the changing nature of medical education and related health fields. Because of the special character of that education, historically taking place in clinical settings alongside the university proper, I treat it as a distinct milieu. A third environment is provided by the state and manifested across the three levels of federal government. The three interacting environments can be represented as a Venn diagram, with the University of Medicine and Dentistry of New Jersey (or any other university with components dedicated to health care) located where the three overlap. These three environments are also understood to incorporate other relevant ones associated with those disputing universities' mission or operation.

Higher Education

The end of World War II and the sudden increase in enrollments that followed from the institution of the GI Bill of Rights brought with it a major expansion of post-secondary education. As a result, higher education became less concentrated on an elite market and more oriented to serving a mass one. That

1 Many of the changes and tensions in higher education discussed can be found globally (Altbach 2011) but the focus here is solely on the United States.

made all schools more vulnerable to tensions between their own autonomous practices and requirements that they display greater public accountability (Schmidtleim and Berdahl 2011). Accountability may be understood as a problem of social control in which the practices and outputs of schools are subject to both internal oversight from administrators and trustees and external oversight from government agencies, professional boards, and independent accrediting bodies.[2]

Even though both existing and new institutions were faced with huge increases in the number of students and the need to quickly develop additional physical plants and teaching staff, the approach to education itself remained locked in tradition. Only with the cultural revolution of the 1960s did the old ways begin to change (Altbach 2011: 24–27). Faculty and students now demanded more say in how they were affected by administrative practices. Universities began to respond to new demands for curricular changes, the introduction of new fields, and the diversification of the students they enrolled and the faculty they hired.

Universities were, as well, pressed to recognize their role as active participants in the larger community in which they existed. Although the link between land-grant universities and their communities had always been present, manifested in the assistance provided to farmers in dealing with agricultural problems and in the timetables built to accommodate the need for their children's presence during agricultural cycles, the new call for university participation was of a different kind. It demanded leadership in the solution of problems of racism, poverty, and urban decline and even of foreign policy.

The period from the mid 1940s through the 1990s also saw unprecedented growth in universities focused on research (Cole 2010). Some universities appeared more successful in furthering research and this would affect relations both within and among universities. Internally, there were growing and enhanced distinctions between those who devoted their time mainly to teaching or to research and, among the latter, between those who were more or less successful in obtaining external funding, leading to concomitant differences in rewards (Salancik and Pfeffer 1974). External validation became tied to the amount of research funding received, the number of publications produced by faculty, and the awards won by faculty and former students. Using such quantitative indicators gave university administrators criteria for engaging in a competitive push to move up in their ranking as a research university.[3]

2 Wiley and Zald (1968) describe and analyze the early growth of these latter organizations.

3 Tuchman (2009) describes this process as it took place within a single state university.

Rankings play an increasingly critical role in public assessments of the prestige of universities and of individual programs within them. They are used, in turn, to attract funding, faculty, and students. There is no agreed upon method for determining rankings and different commentators use different approaches,[4] all of which stimulate some controversy. The best known, and consequently the most influential, of these rankings of undergraduate colleges are produced annually by *U.S. News and World Report* (USNWR), beginning in 1983. USNWR bases its rankings on seven differentially weighted criteria: reputation, student selectivity, faculty resources, graduation and retention rate, financial resources, alumni giving, and graduation rate performance based on a predictive model. Ehrenberg's (2003) review concludes that, as students have become more mobile, and attendance at more highly ranked schools has been demonstrated to have long-lasting economic benefits, colleges and universities have become more competitive in searching for the best students. Although Ehrenberg points out many of the objections to USNWR's methods of weighting and ranking, his primary concern is with the way rankings have contributed to institutional responses that work to the detriment of public higher education. He sees universities' search for the increased enrollment of students with higher test scores undermining attention to educational quality and the special needs of a broader array of students.[5]

Most transformative have been changes in the relation between costs and financing. For students and their families, increases in tuition have led to burdensome debt and universities, both private and public, have responded with offers of financial aid. But the latter still leave universities with the need to find ways to cover these expenses (Ehrenberg 2000). Well-established private universities have relied on income from large endowments but recent years have both eroded the value of those endowments and the income they generate. Public universities must deal with sharply reduced funding from their states (Cohen and Noll 1998: 48–59), a situation that leaves many pessimistic about the ability of such universities to continue as research leaders (e.g., Yudoff 2002).

---

4 For example, Cole (2010) bases his assessment of the top 100 research universities on the Shanghai Jiao Tong University Ranking, measured by the number of prize-winning alumni and faculty, the number of articles published in key journals, and numbers of citations. Kraiger and Abalos (2004), focusing exclusively on industrial-organizational psychology, note the variety of criteria used by others while arguing for the superiority of their assessments, based on student ratings of quality. The most comprehensive evaluations can be found in Goldberger et al. (1995).

5 Ehrenberg notes how administrators can game the system to enhance their ratings. This was anticipated in specific examples given in Chapter 2.

Colleges and universities of all kinds have tended to respond to these financial pressures by adopting models of corporate governance that emphasize efficiency and accountability (Hayes and Wynyard 2002; Tuchman 2009). These foster efforts to evaluate performance, cost-effectiveness, and productivity. Budget cutting has resulted in greater outsourcing of non-academic activities, larger class sizes, and greater use of part-time teachers. Administrators, meanwhile, have assumed more managerial roles, with rewards going disproportionately to those most successful in fund-raising and in enhancing the profile of the university (Ekel and Kazar 2006). If the experiences of Japanese university scientists (Shibayama et al. 2012) are indicative of wider trends, we can anticipate that encouragement of faculty entrepreneurship will negatively affect scientific norms of sharing and cooperation.

From the need for more money, universities are led to search for profit-making opportunities in their midst. Athletics has played this role in the past, although the results have often been incommensurate with the investment and have, at times, introduced corrupting practices. More recently, universities have looked inward, at what goes on in their research labs and centers, and outward, to establish ties with business and industry, for producing increased income. For example, UCLA has created a private foundation, under the supervision of corporate leaders in medicine, engineering, and finance, to take control of its patent and licensing operations (Basken 2013). Derek Bok (2004) warns of great dangers if such commercialization keeps growing. Taking a broader historical perspective, Berman (2011: 2) argues that universities' participation in the marketplace is the result of a new idea, "that scientific and technological innovation serve as engines of economic growth," affecting both policy-makers' and universities' view of their mission.

Regardless of how trends originated, in the current world of higher education changes are reflected in a greater reliance on private money and a greater willingness to allow private interests to dictate what kind of research is emphasized and how results are disseminated. A broad-scale survey on the relations between industry and the university confirms that those relations have grown significantly since the 1970s, with universities their prime instigators. Industry sources of funding tend to be short-term and there is evidence that they are accompanied by restrictions on the dissemination of research findings (Cohen et al. 1998). Specific cases illustrate these trends. Russ Lea (2010), vice president for research at the University of South Alabama, reports on how the oil company BP, following its disastrous oil spill in the Gulf of Mexico, attempted to hire faculty researchers and have them sign contractual agreements that would keep them from making research results available for at least three years. Marion Nestle (2007), professor in the department of Nutrition, Food Studies, and Public Health at New York University, documents the influence of food and beverage companies on both teaching and research in universities and on related professional associations. The connections between pharmaceutical companies and medical device manufacturers are especially critical to medical schools, discussed in the following section.

From the end of World War II to the present, higher education in the United States has undergone major and lasting changes that continue to keep it in a state of uncertainty. Universities and colleges have expanded in number, student body, financial size, and in relations with governments and the broader community. These changes have led them to alter their goals and their governance. To the extent that any of these changes produce stability, they do so only temporarily. Instead, higher education remains in a fluid state, buffeted by internal and external pressures.

Medical Education

All the changes that affect higher education apply as well to the education of medical practitioners and those in allied fields. Rising costs and the search for external funding, the appeals of corporate-style governance, pressures to increase accountability, and competition to increase rankings[6] are all present in medical education. In addition, there are issues specific to medical fields that present universities with unique challenges and the latter are emphasized here. They center on the effects of clinical practice conducted in teaching hospitals and of increased biomedical research. Medical education, in turn, has had an impact on higher education, reflected in the sharp increase in the number of faculty in the health sciences from the mid 1970s to the mid 1990s, a trend unmatched by any other field (Cohen and Noll 1998: 45).

Wherever medicine is taught, either as part of a comprehensive university, like the University of Michigan, or as a medical center complex that includes allied fields, like the University of California at San Francisco, it holds a dominating position in relation to other health-related fields. It is from its status as a profession that medicine enjoys unprecedented prestige (Nakeo and Treas 1992), despite some decline in recent years (Pescosolido et al. 2001).[7] Members

---

6 Among published sources of medical school rankings, Fischman et al. (2008: 8–11) describe variations in teaching, curriculum, research orientation, and reputation and how these affect graduates' choices of residency. Stoll (2004) gives rankings based on student surveys.

7 Since my emphasis is on medical schools and the teaching of medicine and related fields, I am, for the most part, sidestepping concern with the profession of medicine

of a profession are bound by a set of values and obligations encouraging cooperation and adherence to common standards of behavior. A profession is then accorded authority because of its claim to be the repository of expert knowledge. In the case of medicine, that authority has given it unusual power over the entire field of health. "Health services are organized around professional authority, and their basic structure is constituted by the dominance of a single profession over a variety of other, subordinate professions" (Freidson 2006: xi). As a consequence, most of the discussion that follows is from the perspective of medicine.

Although the Flexner Report (1910) had promoted the ideal of teacher-researcher-clinician in medical schools, it is an ideal increasingly difficult to achieve. Unlike other academic fields, where teaching takes place in classrooms and laboratories, teaching in medicine takes place additionally in hospitals and clinics concomitantly with the treatment of patients. Each role has the potential for taking over virtually all available time in ways that are even more troublesome than the tension between research and teaching in research universities generally. Despite arguments about the necessity for physician-scientists, there is serious concern about the difficulty of sustaining this tandem role (Pizzo 2009).

Clinical practice raises unique issues about remuneration. For all university faculty members, salaries are set yearly, whether through negotiations or contractual terms of employment. Normally, earnings from publications produced while faculty members are under university contract are treated as belonging to the individuals who wrote them. New products and processes that may be patented are generally subject to prior contractual understandings about to whom profits belong and how they may be divided. But in the case of clinical practice, medical faculty receives, along with a base salary, an additional agreed-upon amount tied to the number of patients seen and the procedures performed. This is possible because the additional amounts come, not from the university's budget, but from patients' payment for services. The practice of payment for clinical services began with the advent of Medicare and Medicaid that, along with an increase in employer-supported health insurance, gave new incentives to clinical faculty to devote themselves to patient care (Cluff 1983). Typically, clinical fees are collected by the university which deducts about 16 percent for administrative purposes and then allots about 42 percent for physician compensation (Cohen 1998: 151). Even the calculation of physicians' base salary differs from that of other faculty through the use of a

itself, which is increasingly under pressure from market forces it is unable to control (Light 2010).

twelve-month calendar year rather than the more usual nine month. The justification is that the responsibilities of physician-faculty are undiminished, regardless of the university's normal timetable.

Relations between faculty and university hospitals are complicated by their monetary links in ways additional to the issue of remuneration. Increasingly, provision of medical services make up a significant part of campus funding[8] at the same time as those services may be more expensive than ones offered at community hospitals (Cohen 1998: 147). In a highly competitive world, and one in which income from patient services is declining, university hospitals finds themselves in a critical situation as they search for alternative organizational forms (e.g., Ginzberg 1996). Their difficulties are compounded by major changes occurring in health care delivery systems in general (Fennell and Adams 2011: 212–214).

Although medical education has always had socially significant goals, those related to under-served populations raise new questions and new tensions about the allocation of resources (Walsh[9] 1971c: 787). Particularly during economic downturns, when both external funding is cut and more patients are uninsured, teaching hospitals are in the troubling position of drawing resources away from other parts of their universities. Mangan (2009) reports that "Major teaching hospitals account for 6 percent of the nation's hospitals but provide 41 percent of charity care." This situation becomes even more acute where teaching hospitals are located in inner city areas with large numbers of low income and uninsured patients (Kastor 2004: 30).

In the period after the mid 1940s, the content of medical education changed through a huge expansion in biomedical science and research (Sheps and Seipp 1972; Walsh 1971a). On the positive side, research helped introduce new diagnostic tools and treatments. Emphasis on a stronger scientific orientation led to calls for evidence-based medicine. Yet, overall, there have been only selective consequences for how medicine is practiced. As Grob and Horvitz (2010: 31–32) demonstrate through six case studies, "Etiological theories that have little or no basis in fact, diagnoses that lack reliability or validity, and therapies whose efficacy is at best problematic and at worst dangerous are all too common." The disconnect between what is taught in medical schools and the ability of practitioners to apply its principles demonstrates the difficulty of translating continuously changing scientific findings,

8 For example, medical schools reported that, in 1993–94, such services contributed almost 50 percent of their revenues (Ganem et al. 1995).

9 Walsh's 1971 reports on the problems of medical education at Stanford University were an insightful analysis of then current issues that remain relevant to present day conditions.

communicated in classrooms and laboratories, with the routine demands of medical practice.

Current problems in the practice of medicine have many of their origins in the educational experiences of students. Socialization into the medical profession begins not only with the formal curriculum but also in the implicit messages conveyed through the informal and hidden curriculum (Ludmerer 1999). Those who have gone through the process of learning to become physicians recount the conflicting pulls between scientific and humanistic medicine (Conrad 1988). Ethical values are largely conveyed through the hidden curriculum, where students observe the kinds of actions that are rewarded, often in opposition to formally stated ethical positions (Hundert 1996; Hafferty and Franks 1994). But when calls for reform are raised and then fail, this can be tied to the larger environment of which medical education is but one component (Ludmerer 2012).

Expansion of biomedical science has also had implications within health care education for financing, departmental specialization, clinical training, and relations with external bodies. The vast investment of public money from both federal and state governments has reinforced the departmentalization of medicine. Different fields display different skills in raising and making money, accentuating tensions between clinical practice and biomedical research (Walsh 1971b: 654). These trends make it common to "bootleg" the costs of clinical training into more lucrative sources of funding (Walsh 1971a: 553). They also redistribute the bases of power away from departmental deans to the most successful money raisers (Walsh 1971a) as well as to central administrations.

Into this volatile milieu of declining resources and conflicting roles, the entry of pharmaceutical[10] and medical device manufacturers opens additional opportunities for conflicts of interest (Brennan et al. 2006).[11] That entry has affected all levels of university life, beginning with medical students receiving meals, gifts, and industry-sponsored educational materials (Austad and Kesselheim 2011). While companies may supply new research funding and educational support, they can also compromise the integrity of research findings

10 Light et al. (2013) describe the pernicious effects following from the institutional corruption of the pharmaceutical industry.

11 Some of these conflicts of interest are manifested in the practice of medicine generally. For example, pharmaceutical companies use marketing tools targeted to physicians to increase prescriptions for drugs (Weiss 2010), clinical practice guidelines developed for the American Psychiatric Association are influenced by the financial ties between pharmaceutical companies and the authors of those guidelines (Cosgrove et al. 2009), and the Heart Rhythm Society has welcomed sponsorships by device makers (Ornstein and Weber 2011).

and can influence faculty to promote their products. Beyond the usual marketing techniques of strategically-directed gifts, companies may offer faculty rewards that, in addition to monetary ones, enhance faculty prestige through speaking engagements and the publication of articles that have, in fact, been ghostwritten by company employees (Silverman 2010). They may go so far as to intimidate faculty to prevent the dissemination of unfavorable research findings (United States Senate Committee on Finance 2007).

The egregiousness of these practices have led to protests by medical students (Kluger 2009), counter-measures by universities (e.g., Stanford University 2006/2010), and congressional hearings (United States Senate Committee on Finance 2010). Yet, in reviewing policies and changes advocated by the National Institutes of Health (NIH), the major funder of biomedical research, Greenberg (2010) remains skeptical that that agency has found any effective ways of policing conflicts of interest. Medical schools may be in a more difficult situation, caught between their desire for increased funding and the added prestige from faculty accomplishments and their reluctance to use sanctions that might affect either of these. For example, even after pharmaceutical company GlaxoSmithKline admitted that Professor of Psychiatry Martin Keller had co-authored an article (or had published a ghostwritten one) that falsely claimed to demonstrate the beneficial effects of its drug Paxil for adolescents suffering from depression, Brown University, where Dr Keller was chair of his department, took no action against him (Luthra 2012). The absence of overt signs of undue influence may still raise suspicions about connections between faculty and industry. This was exemplified in the case of the dean of Weill Cornell Medical College. Although never accused of using her positions as a director in a large pharmaceutical company and in a laboratory equipment company, from which she obtained sizable salaries, to promote their products in her school, her connections strongly implied ethical questions (Stein 2012).

All of these sources of tension are endemic to academic medical centers in the United States and there is little to differentiate them in these respects, whether they are part of state-supported systems or independent. Assessing the trends affecting medical education by the 1980s, Cluff (1983: 2934) concluded that, "Of these three important elements of medical schools, medical care and medical research have developed 'elephantiasis' while medical education seems to have atrophied." This devaluation of teaching has produced frustrations among faculty. Even the apparent emphasis on medical care has not come about without arousing similar frustrations from faculty who do not see organizational practices as commensurate with their own values concerning patient care (Pololi et al. 2009). Developments in medicine and medical education, described by Walsh (1971a) following World War II, have continued to grow, bringing with them organizational problems augmented by financial shortfalls and inequities, by the intrusion of corporate interests with their own agendas, and by concerns about the integrity of scientific output.[12]

The Role of the State

Although, constitutionally, education may be under the purview of state governments, that has not prevented significant federal interventions into higher education (Mumper et al. 2011: 114–117). During the nineteenth century, federal involvement was channeled to individual states through the Morrill Land Grant Act of 1862, which led to the establishment of programs and universities expected to help in western expansion. During the twentieth century, federal intervention was more direct and aimed at expanding student enrolment. Most recently, the Economic Stimulus Bill provided relief to states and allowed the continued funding of public universities that would have otherwise been penalized by the economic downturn.

For medical schools, the federal government has been the major source of funding for research and development, increasingly regularly from the 1970s through the 1990s, when it began to decline. In order to obtain such funding, researchers, whether individually or in groups, must submit proposals that are then subject to peer review. In addition to the direct costs associated with the research, normally covering personnel, equipment, and supplies, universities may charge indirect costs associated with overhead, with the latter often a matter of contention between universities and the federal government. Indirect costs vary among universities with a tendency toward higher costs among medical schools (Noll and Rogerson 1998: 132–134). The grant process is highly competitive and most rewards go to the top 100 research universities, both private and public. In addition, since the 1970s, the federal government has been reluctant to fund equipment and facilities. These characteristics have led many universities to go directly to Congress and lobby for special earmarks. If the peer review process appeared to favor elite universities as part of an "old boys' network," the newer lobbying process raises concerns about the diminution of scientific standards and a move to politicize research (Mumper et al. 2011: 128–131).

A second major way that the federal government has an impact on the financing of medical schools is through Medicare and Medicaid payments that

12 A review of biomedical and life-science research articles retracted showed that two-thirds of them were retracted because of misconduct, primarily fraud (Fang et al. 2012).

are critical for the ongoing support of teaching hospitals. Medicare is totally federally-funded and available to all who are covered by Social Security and reach a stipulated age; Medicaid is means-tested, receives some state funding, and is state-administered. Both programs set out standards of care, among them the physical presence of the attending physician for whom reimbursement is requested. Because the Department of Health and Human Services already pays for the training of residents at teaching hospitals, asking for reimbursement for their services can be viewed as a form of double billing, an area of contention between universities and government. Meanwhile, teaching hospitals compete with community and private hospitals for patients and payments while remaining vulnerable to changing formulas for reimbursement.

In contrast with the federal government, states have unquestioned authority over the life of public universities. They have served as their creators, funders, employers, and overseers of their governance. How active they are in these roles has varied over time and by state. Oversight, in particular, reflects the tensions between demands for university autonomy and public accountability, tensions that become more acute during times of fiscal crisis (McGuinness 2011: 151). Oversight is assigned to a board, typically appointed by the governor, with possible input from the legislature,[13] that serves much like the board of directors of a non-profit agency. Board responsibility may cover all public universities and colleges in the state,[14] be divided by type of institution, or confined to a single campus (Kerr and Gade 1989). Board responsibilities include, but are not confined to, planning, budgeting, allocating resources, and personnel policies. Boards differ, depending on whether they are structured to emphasize governance or coordination. Governing boards hire the chief executives and set personnel policy. Coordinating boards deal with state-wide concerns with higher education and evaluate and set compensation only for the executive officer and staff that serves the board (McGuinness 2011: 144–148.)

Institutional arrangements that connect public universities with state governments are also subject to change. Volkwein and Malik (1997) looked at the top tier of public universities and found that, from 1983 to 1995, those universities gained in both academic and administrative autonomy. More recently,

13 The University of Illinois system exemplified one with an elected Board of Trustees (Nowlan et al. 1984). It changed in 1995 to one appointed by the Governor. Election was then confined to student member trustees.

14 For example, the University System of Georgia, the fourth largest such system in the country, is governed by a Board of Regents appointed by the Governor, who is also an ex officio member of the Board. It oversees 35 public institutions, setting goals, allocating state funds, and appointing the chancellor who heads the system (Fincher 2003).

however, there is a perception that change has been in the direction of increasing state oversight, as in the case of Florida (OPPAGA 2010), or North Dakota, where it was in response to a series of scandals (Kelderman 2012).

Up until the 1990s, the single largest source of funding for public universities came from their state governments. Since then, state contributions have declined, forcing universities both to cut back on programs and personnel and to look to other sources of revenue. One explanation for the decline is that appropriations are tied to state revenues and, as the latter have been affected by the economic downturn begun in the mid 1990s, so too have allocations to public universities. A second factor associates Republican governors with decline (Cohen and Noll 1996: 53–58), a reflection of increased partisan conflict over budget-cutting. Yet another factor is tied to the burgeoning costs in managing university hospitals, leading to remedies that loosen state control and look to the private sector for models (Schmidt 1996).

The effects of state structures on the universities they control have been scrutinized by a number of researchers but often without finding strong or consistent relations. For example, Lowry (2001) found that, in states where centralized political control is stronger and where trustees are selected by non-academics, universities charge lower prices. But Nicholson-Crotty and Meier (2003) observed that, while different kinds of boards were differentially associated with the ability to insulate universities from political influences, they were not able to answer "exactly how structure affects political influence." Volkwein and Malik (1997) see the connection between states' oversight capability and actual control to be "idiosyncratic." McGuinness (2011) moves away from focusing on specific structural characteristics to frame the relations between state governments and their universities as strained, the result of increasing demands, economic limitations, resistance to administrative change typical of most universities, and the absence of stable political leadership in the states.

Although it might be assumed that the ties between state governments and public universities do not leave room for any impact from local governments, this is not the case. Local interest is high, given the residential origins of most students, the job opportunities campuses provide to residents, and the business opportunities for surrounding communities. Local officials can be influential in establishing a welcoming setting for campuses, including where they are located.[15] The importance of the local connection is also evident from

15 For example, Mayor Richard Daley was a principal actor in selecting the Near Westside location for what was then called the Chicago Circle campus of the University of Illinois (Rosen 1980).

the interests expressed by legislators. From his study of the University of Illinois and Penn State, Lane (2007: 626–627) observes:

> Even though the institutions...are chartered by the state, are funded by the state, and proclaim national and international missions, they continue to exhibit strong entanglements with the local communities in which they operate. In fact, one of the more interesting findings of this study is the proposition that the larger the institution (in terms of the number of campuses), the more opportunities for local oversight to occur existed.

This overview of the role of the state makes clear that it involves governments at all levels. Higher education and its medical component share an interdependence with the full range of governmental levels that is strong but variable, differing among states and over time. Individual universities are then left facing a vital yet unstable environment.

Anticipated Impact

The conditions and environments of higher education and the forms they take in medical education, along with the environment provided by the state in all its complexity, surround the decisions made and the actions available to every state-supported and, only to a lesser extent with respect to state impact, non-state-supported academic medical centers. Yet, beyond tracing broad trends in these relationships, it is not clear precisely what their impact may be on individual universities or how the latter may be led to adopt illegal and unethical practices. I explore those possibilities by outlining a general approach to when and how organizational misconduct might be encouraged.

The most fundamental finding emerging from the current chapter is the extent of change in higher education that began in the mid 1940s and assumed new trajectories after the late 1960s, again in the early 1990s, and later, in the early 2000s. It is change that has helped refashion medical education with respect to its nature and to the quantity and distribution of resources available to it. Among the major consequences for any organization experiencing such change is a heightened state of uncertainty. One consequence is the appearance of new norms, attuned to changed conditions, alongside the durability of old ones with which they may come in conflict (Granovetter 2007: 167). Another related outcome is the appearance of new structures that, depending on how they take shape, may create new opportunities for corrupt forms of influence

(Prechel and Morris 2010: 334). Within academic health centers, competing norms and structures emerged from the push for greater administrative control; contention among standards for teaching, research, and patient care; and priorities assigned to them. Scott (2004) sees comparable changes leading to competition among professional, state, and managerial approaches in facing problems within the health care industry. From such competition, I hypothesize that

> H_1: Changes that result in competing normative and structural responses open opportunities for corruption.

Uncertainty stimulates an ever-expanding competitive search for resources of all kinds (Pfeffer and Salancik 1978). Resources may be financial, ones of power and influence; or those involving status, standards, and values. Competition is the normal world in which individuals, groups, and organizations (as well as states) operate as they look for advantages in protecting and increasing resources. The manner in which that competition takes place is shaped by its context and the norms developed to constrict what is acceptable and permissible. At times, competition provides incentives to overstep formal or informal limits and become corrupt (Baucus 1994: 704–705). Incentives may arise from the environment in which organizations operate, within organizations themselves, or from the cognitions and choices made by individuals (Vaughan 1999). Incentives can then be a powerful influence on unethical behavior (Tenbrunsel 1998). Jensen (2001), for example, notes how corporate budgeting practices that offer performance-based incentives create conditions that encourage gaming the system.

> H_2: Incentives to gain scarce resources can encourage the use of illegal or unethical means.

No matter how widespread the incentives arising from resource dependence, it is the opportunities for acting on them that are critical. These emerge from the embeddedness of institutions in social relations that may sustain, modify, or disrupt those institutions. Just as "embeddedness...stresses...the role of concrete personal relations and structures ('networks') of such relations in generating trust and discouraging malfeasance" (Granovetter 1985: 490), it may do the opposite, depending on the nature of the social structures present (Granovetter 1985: 493). Corruption may take place in market-like structures, where transactions are impersonal and often transitory, or in network-like structures, where continuing ties of obligation predominate (Granovetter

2007: 161–162). Prechel (2000) expands the application of embeddedness by taking into account the ties between organizations and the state. In other words, opportunities for corruption can emerge from embeddedness in either of three kinds of interactions.

University medical centers are embedded in market-like relations through the wide variety of goods and services they purchase or contract for, like office, laboratory, and hospital supplies; the building, acquisition, and maintenance of their physical facilities; provision of services to community groups, patients, and students linked to payments for those services; and even some aspects of the recruitment of faculty, staff, and students. Network-like structures are built on values of obligation that characterize relations with some expectation of continuity. These may emerge from relations between administrators and employees, faculty and students, medical personnel and patients and may extend, as well, to those involving university administrators with politicians and government personnel or even administrators with commercial vendors. Political embeddedness arises from relations between a university and the state as well as other supervisory or regulatory agents. When embeddedness works in positive ways, relations are sustained by conceptions and standards of fairness that operate even among those with unequal power. In all three forms of embeddedness, opportunities for corruption can be understood through analogy with a principal-agent relation, where the principal controls benefits and costs that offer opportunity for rent-seeking behavior (that is, ways to maximize self-interest) and where the agent has discretion to allow rent-seekers unfair, including illegal, access to those benefits (Rose-Ackerman 1999: 9). Moreover, in settings where individuals may be called upon to make rapid decisions, by interpreting rules under conditions of possible danger and without close supervision, opportunities are ripe for a range of deviant behaviors (Van Maanen 1972). This leads to anticipating that

> H_3: opportunities for corruption appear when embedded relations are controlled by agents with discretion to allow unfair access to benefits.

Dealing, as we are, with systemic corruption, relegates to a tangential problem behavior that seeks benefits for particular individuals. Of greater concern is the distortion of goals that occurs through an emphasis on benefits for the organization, regardless of how these are achieved. When top-level administrators set goals for those at lower levels of the organization that can only be achieved through cutting corners, they foster a culture that encourages illegal or unethical behavior and may even direct subordinates to engage in such behavior. The longer such activities continue, the greater the likelihood they will become institutionalized into the practices of the organization (Greve et al. 2010: 75). The prediction then is that, in setting goals, administrators become responsible for how limits are set on what are acceptable actions and the culture that develops to sustain those actions. In effect,

> H_4: when management places attainment of organizational goals above the selection of legal or ethical means to do so, it sets the stage for organizational misconduct.

The conditions of uncertainty facing organizations dependent on their environments for resources ensure that they operate with reduced autonomy (Pfeffer and Salancik 1978). The efforts of university medical centers to overcome this limitation have led to increased bureaucratization through an emphasis on centralized authority and formalized measures of efficiency along with a reduction in collegial forms of authority and shared governance. The functioning of medical centers that must deal with their increased organizational complexity and the contention that may follow is tied to the nature and distribution of relevant information. Where information is limited, obfuscated, or deliberately hidden, opportunities for malfeasance increase. This general observation is tied to arguments that transparency serves as a counter to corruption (e.g., Rose-Ackerman 1999; Transparency International 2001). Lindstedt and Naurin (2010) confirm the deterrent effects of transparency in their cross-national analysis, adding that it is important that citizens have the capacity to act on the basis of information received. They remind us of Bentham's assertion that,

> The greater the number of temptations to which the exercise of political power is exposed, the more necessary is it to give to those who possess it, the most powerful reasons for resisting them. But there is no reason more constant and more universal than the superintendence of the public.
>
> BENTHAM 1999: 29

It follows from these arguments that, in university medical centers,

> H_5: the lack of transparency offers a prime opportunity for malfeasance.

Where competition for resources helps define relations among units within a single organization, the resulting rivalry is difficult to compensate for with coordinating mechanisms. For example, a hierarchical structure that results in centralization will have a negative impact on encouraging internal knowledge-sharing (Tsai 2002). Instead, competitive internal cultures develop that emphasize their own goals and interests (Schmidt and Kochan 1972). This can build both incentives and opportunities to resort to misconduct. From this we can anticipate that

> H_6: when internal competition inhibits building a collective identity, conditions arise that encourage deviant behavior.

Organizational complexity increases the likelihood that there will be actors with unique access to information. Scheppelle (1993) examined how this occurs when the stock market is manipulated through inside information. Such access gives actors autonomy and, where there are structural holes created through non-reciprocated contacts, they may exploit their information for their own benefit (Burt 1992). Prechel and Morris (2010: 335) expand on Burt by pointing out how structural holes can be illegitimately exploited to conceal risks or bend rules. In university medical centers, possessing asymmetric information may give rise to opportunities for corruption by allowing information to be hidden, distorted, or otherwise obscured through building layers of complexity. We can anticipate then that,

> H_7: structural holes give opportunities to falsify and distort information.

A further way in which the nature of information can create openings for corrupt behavior is tied to the costs of obtaining or verifying it. As Vaughan (1982: 375) points out, when the costs of obtaining information independently are high, organizations and individuals may rely on the signals they receive from those who originate it. But those signals may be altered, either through individual initiative or from organizational practices. One example is when university teaching hospitals, in order to provide Medicaid services, submit evidence of their eligibility (signals) that are often not verified. Opportunities then emerge to manipulate the required data. In general,

> H_8: when obtaining firsthand information is cumbersome and there is, instead, reliance for that information on organizational signaling, opportunities can arise to manipulate signals in order to gain unfair advantage.

The dominance of medicine over other fields and the hierarchy of privilege associated with it can be anticipated to produce a model of organization that discourages critical examination of behavior generally. Dunn and Schweitzer (2005: 52) characterize this as a "culture of unquestioning obedience to leadership" that serves to insulates administrative practices from oversight. The result is an organizational culture that

> H_9: allows deference to flourish and deviant behavior to be unchallenged.

Explaining Organizational Corruption

This chapter has argued that major changes affecting higher education, augmented by those affecting academic medical centers, have created conditions where adapting to them takes place in uncertain and competitive environments. Given dependence on their environments for resources, universities may experience the pressures they face as incentives to adopt illegal or unethical means to acquire those resources. From incentives they may move to find opportunities to act on them. Such opportunities arise from new and conflicting norms and structural arrangements that allow for discretion in allocating rewards. Opportunities appear as well when there are impediments to free and undistorted flows of information. Opportunities also emerge where internal cultures discourage questioning authority and impede commitments to ethical standards that reach beyond narrow segments of the organization.

The literature on organizations is the source for the series of hypotheses about when academic medical centers will become corrupted. Their ability to effectively explain UMDNJ's legal and ethical lapses into corruption are tested in the following two chapters. Chapter 4 applies them to UMDNJ's core organizational structure and Chapter 5, to UMDNJ's network structure.

CHAPTER 4

UMDNJ's Core Organization

Selecting Actors and Activities

UNDNJ was New Jersey's only publicly-funded comprehensive provider of training to large numbers of health care professionals and of services affecting the population's health. It carried out its responsibilities on campuses and affiliated health centers and hospitals spread over the state. The stresses UMDNJ faced in fulfilling its many roles were placed into a larger and more general context in Chapter 3 by taking into account the multiple and interacting problems facing higher education in the US and the special ones facing the health fields, all mediated by relations with the state. In this chapter we move back to UMDNJ and its place in New Jersey to confront the complexity of its organization and governance. By translating the general problems of medical education into the experiences of one medical center, we can begin to isolate those features that contributed to UMDNJ's vulnerability to corruption. Once the specific analysis is completed in this and the following two chapters, translation can move in the opposite direction, using UMDNJ's experiences to illuminate processes of institutional corruption affecting higher education in general.

Although organizational theorists and students of higher education (e.g., Birnbaum 1988; Kerr 2001; Tolbert 1985; Cohen and March 1986) demonstrate that there is no single best way to describe a university's organization and governance, they agree on the importance of distinguishing between the university's principal functions. I follow their guidance by focusing on the administrative and academic positions that were at the core of how UMDNJ functioned. These are identified as all positions covered under UMDNJ's name and they are examined with respect to activities and responsibilities, relations with others, and history. History is highlighted to pick up the time when practices were institutionalized, periods of volatility, and the identity of incumbents who faced or contributed to either. By not imposing any expectations, the description that follows allows the contours of relationships to emerge from the data.

I have chosen to distinguish the University's core from its larger network by placing the Board of Trustees into the network because it was the principal oversight agency. This results in emphasizing the nature of the latter role, distinct from the University's day to day operations. Omitting the trustees from the core is a judgment on my part and does not deny the efficacy of more traditional approaches to UMDNJ's structure, which put the trustees at the top of the organization, found, for example, in the report on the state of the University (Commission on Health Sciences 2004: 108).

Core Actors

President

The President was the University's public face, representing it before the Board of Trustees, other government agencies, and affected individuals and organizations. Within his office, the academic and administrative activities of the University came together. The President was formally hired by the trustees, who were themselves appointed by the state Governor. In practice, the Governor had been the major agent in appointing presidents.

In 1966, in what was still the College of Medicine and Dentistry of New Jersey, a period of initial organization began under the presidency of Robert R. Cadmus, M.D. Major changes came in 1971 with Governor William Cahill's appointment of Stanley S. Bergen, Jr., M.D.,[1] the person who is always considered the first president. Over 27 years, Dr. Bergen built the University into a multi-campus giant by exerting tight control over its administration and development.

Dr. Bergen's retirement in 1998 was associated with rumors that Governor Christie Whitman had let it be known that it was time for him to leave. According to a person close to the events, the chairman of the Board of Trustees, who owed his position to the Governor, was instructed to engineer Dr. Bergen's removal. Although acknowledging that he was not close to the Governor, Dr. Bergen denied that he was under pressure to leave. However, he had been a party to at least one public clash with her in the University's unsuccessful court challenge that opposed the state for allowing Saint Barnabas Health Care System, located in Livingston NJ, to operate in Newark as the Children's Hospital of New Jersey (Scott 1998a).

---

1 Dr. Bergen, a New Jersey native, graduated from Princeton and took his medical degree from Columbia University. He became interested in community medicine early in his career, serving as chief of community medicine at Brooklyn-Cumberland Medical Center and then briefly, under Mayor John Lindsay, as vice-president for medical and professional affairs at the New York City Health and Hospitals Corporation. It was from this last position that he was invited to assume the presidency of the College of Medicine and Dentistry of New Jersey (CMDNJ).

Based on recommendations from a professional search company, the University's own search committee selected three finalists to replace Dr. Bergen. Although never officially confirmed, the Board of Trustees was said to have offered the position to Dr. Willis Maddrey, former president of the American College of Physicians and vice president for clinical affairs at the University of Southwestern Medical Center. Another finalist, Bruce Vladeck, who holds a Ph.D. in political science and is a recognized expert on health care policy, earlier withdrew from consideration and accepted the position of vice president at Mount Sinai Medical School in Manhattan (Scott 1998b). Surveying its actions, Dr. Bergen told the Board of Trustees that none of the three candidates under consideration was worthy enough to assume the presidency (Fisher 1998).

On the day following the breakdown of negotiations with Dr. Maddrey, Stuart D. Cook, M.D., who had founded the University's department of neuroscience, was asked to take over (Stewart 1998). Dr. Cook was initially a member of the search committee for a new president but resigned from the committee when he was asked to serve as acting president in July 1998. In November, Governor Whitman appointed him president (Campbell 1998). On taking office, Dr. Cook said his goal was to enhance the university's reputation by commitment to research and teaching. But one person interviewed, who had access to administrative practices, described Dr. Cook as "not really running the place," a view echoed by others. Dr. Cook, who came into conflict with the newly elected Democratic Governor, James E. McGreevey, over the Governor's unrealized plan to merge UMDNJ with Rutgers University and the New Jersey Institute of Technology, resigned in 2004 (James 2004).

Governor McGreevey's next move was to appoint John Petillo[2] as interim president. The Governor had previously named Dr. Petillo to the Board of Trustees, where he became chairman. At the same time as Dr. Petillo took over in an interim capacity, the Board was also considering a distinguished medical researcher for the presidency – Allen Spiegel, director of the National Institute of Diabetes and Digestive and Kidney Diseases at the National Institute of Health. Adding their voices to the debate, three faculty members, Professors Frohman, Katz, and Goldman (2004), made a public plea in the Newark *Star-Ledger* for a nation-wide search aimed at "finding the best leadership available and making sure that leadership can act unfettered by political considerations." But recognizing the advantage enjoyed by Dr. Petillo, the *Star-Ledger* (2004), in

2 Dr. Petillo's doctoral degree is in counseling and his administrative experience was gained as chancellor of Seton Hall University and as chief executive of Blue Cross Blue Shield of New Jersey.

turn, editorialized that "It is reasonable to ask whether other candidates for president looked at that shuffle, saw a stacked deck and decided not to apply." Dr. Petillo's position was made official in November 2004 and he was formally installed as president in April 2005.[3] After the University's troubles surfaced and its Board of Trustees entered into agreements with the United States Attorney Chris Christie for deferred prosecution and placement under a federal monitor in December 2005, described in Chapter 2, Dr. Petillo was pressured to resign by Governor Corzine (Heyboer and Sherman 2006).

The void left by Dr. Petillo's resignation was temporarily filled by Dr. Denise V. Rodgers, chief of staff and executive vice-president. Dr. Rodgers is an expert on health disparities affecting minorities and was appointed executive vice president by Dr. Petillo in 2005. She had also been associate dean for community health and professor of family medicine in the Robert Wood Johnson Medical School.

Governor Jon Corzine, who took office in 2005, now had his opportunity to affect the University's administration. He did so by appointing an interim president, Bruce C. Vladeck, in March 2006. Dr. Vladeck, as noted earlier, had been a finalist to succeed Dr. Bergen.[4] However, whatever motivation Dr. Vladeck had to seek the presidency as a permanent position faded when the federal monitor accused him of trying to cover over evidence of misdeeds (Stern 2006c: 24–25; Kocieniewski 2006c). Shortly after, he resigned and returned to his former position at Ernst and Jones.

The Board of Trustees now had the task of finding a permanent president. This activity was always among its official duties, but, under prior administrations, the Governor played the most active role, something that Governor Corzine may no longer have found as attractive. The Board appointed a search committee made up of UMDNJ members and associates and headed by Dr. Harold T. Shapiro, former president of Princeton University and now a member of the UMDNJ's Board of Trustees. The Trustees approved the

---

3 Once officially recognized, Dr. Petillo hosted an elaborate celebration with family and friends, among whom were Richard Codey, who was completing his first day as Acting Governor (Patterson 2004).

4 At the time of his appointment Dr. Vladeck was executive director of Health Sciences Advisory Services at Ernst and Jones. His experience included serving as administrator of Health Care Financing Administration in the U.S. Department of Health and Human Services between 1993 and 1997. He came with some knowledge of local politics from his term as assistant commissioner of NJ's Department of Health from 1979 to 1982. Professional recognition was validated by election to the Institute of Medicine of the National Academy of Sciences in 1986.

appointment of Dr. William F. Owen, Jr., who was then Chancellor of the University of Tennessee Health Sciences Center.[5] Dr. Owen officially became president in 2007 (Kocieniewski 2007). His tenure was marked by low key efforts to calm controversy and repair the image of the University. But from the perspective of some observers, he was considered distant and ineffective, unpopular with faculty and lacking in political savvy. He resigned in 2012, once it was evident that the latest Governor, Chris Christie, would not allow the University to continue in its current form. Dr. Rodgers was once again called upon, first to become interim President and later President, an office she held up to the time UMDNJ was formally dissolved.

All presidential administrations shared two principal tasks. The first was coordination of all activities that dealt with academic affairs affecting students and faculty. The second was oversight of all administrative activities involved in running a complex organization. These included the building and grounds that made up the campuses, safety, legal responsibilities, publicity and lobbying, and contacts with government agencies and the public. As the University grew and presidential administrations changed, positions and their lines of authority changed as well. For the most part, I will be focusing on times when each of the two principal areas was headed by a senior vice president who, in turn, oversaw an extensive hierarchy of offices.

The University and its hospitals and research centers were housed in physical plants that could be expanded and always needed maintenance and repair. Its faculty, employees, patients, and students required services dependent on equipment and food. Requisitioning support services came under the mandate of the Senior Vice President for Administration and Finance and compliance with university policy was supervised by the Associate Vice President for Support Services. The latter office's objective was to prevent individual faculty or staff from encumbering the University with contractual payments. Even more elaborate procedures were in place for purchases. In the case of purchases over $5000 but under $24,000, user departments were required to obtain at least three price quotations. For those over $24,000, the University normally required solicitation of bids. It was possible to obtain waivers for bids under the supervision of the Executive Director for Materials Management who reported to the Vice President for Administration. Criteria for waivers followed New Jersey State Laws 52:34-9 and 52:34-10 and covered such items as perishable food or supplies and the leasing of property under

5 Owen, who held an M.D. from Tufts University, had previously been chief scientist for Baxter Healthcare Corporation and was an expert in kidney disease.

circumstances where there was only a single source or there was need for immediate delivery. But as the examples cited in Chapter 2 indicated, avoidance of bidding requirements was frequent and applied broadly to include how lobbyists were hired.

Under President Bergen, faculty and academic affairs were under the supervision of Executive Vice President Charles Vevier from 1971 to 1983. Dr. Vevier, a historian by training, had been recruited to the new College of Medicine and Dentistry of New Jersey and continued in his post when it became UMDNJ. When Fred Hammond served as Executive Vice President, from 1986 to 1997, his duties were less broad and he resigned under pressure (Scott 1998c). Bergen's initial appointment as Senior Vice President for Administration was Paul Gazzero, who was placed on leave in 1990 amid rumors that he was responsible for financial problems then facing the University (Whitlow 1990a). At the time, the Senior Vice President for Academic Affairs was Dr. Richard Reynolds, who was followed by Dr. Paul Larson in 1989. Dr. Larson had been encouraged to leave his position as dean of the Louisiana State University Medical School with one inducement a loan package of $567,000 guaranteed to him by UMDNJ. With time, there was some expectation that Larson might succeed Dr. Bergen (Fisher 1998). But relations with the President deteriorated and Dr. Larson was placed on paid leave in 1997 and then fired the following year.

Under President Stuart Cook, academic responsibilities were assigned to Robert Saporito, D.D.S., then Dean of the School of Dentistry. Saporito served first in an acting capacity and then became Senior Vice President for Academic Affairs. He was asked to resign in 2006, after the federal monitor presented allegations that Saporito had abused his expense account (Stern 2006a: 69–75). Although Saporito was known to be involved in Republican politics, he did not have the same direct connections as did the Senior Vice President for Administration and Finance, James Archibald, who was appointed in 1997 after leaving the administration of Governor Whitman. Two other former Whitman officials also played a prominent role under President Cook–John Ekarius, vice president for government and public affairs, and Louis Goetting, vice president for administration. It was these three former Whitman appointees who were said to hold the real power in the Cook administration.

Archibald, to be shadowed by allegations of involvement in Medicare and Medicaid overbilling and blamed as an architect of the scheme to hire cardiologists to induce them to send patients to University Hospital, described in Chapter 2, resigned in 2002 to take a position at Drexel University. His departure went along with a generous "golden parachute," a practice that also benefitted Ekarius and Goetting[6] (Sherman and Margolin 2005). Although Whitman was no longer governor, her successor, Republican Governor Donald T. DiFrancesco, could still offer her three former employees some political cover.

In addition to positions overseeing the two principal administrative functions under the President's authority, there needed to be legal oversight to ensure that the multiple contractual relations involving all the components of the University were in compliance with federal and state laws. In this capacity, Vivian Sanks King took office in 1993 as Vice President for Legal Management and general counsel for the University under the presidency of Dr. Bergen. Her downfall came with allegations of double billing Medicaid, a practice that her legal department knew about for at least three years without taking any action. When Sanks King did hire an outside law firm to research the matter, its final report was altered from earlier drafts and excused the University from any obligation to report the double billing to Medicaid. U.S. Attorney Christie blamed Sanks King and her department for the absence of proper oversight and demanded that she be fired (Reisinger 2006; Margolin and Heyboer 2005e). She was asked to resign by President Petillo in 2005. However, no evidence of criminal intent was ever found and finally, in a letter from the U.S. Attorney's office dated June 10, 2008, she was cleared of all charges[7] (Margolin 2009).

Through much of its history, the presidential office was one of concentrated power exerted over all the academic and administrative responsibilities that made up UMDNJ. In addition, power extended outside the University proper, reaching into surrounding communities and touching political officeholders. Externally-linked political power was, however, a double-edged sword, with each president dependent on the governor who appointed him and each resigning under the tenure of a different governor, usually of the opposite political party. The president best able to exercise the full range of authority and who, in fact, shaped the office's growth and development, was Stanley

---

6 Of the three former Whitman administrators, only Goetting escaped being called by federal investigators. He remained in NJ, first as executive vice president at Brookdale Community College in Monmouth County (Sherman and Margolin 2005), from which he took early retirement, and then as Cabinet Secretary to Governor Christie. The kinds of severance packages that Goetting enjoyed brought him 1.1 million dollars along with ongoing pension payments (Lagerkvist 2011).

7 At the time he was running for Governor, Christie still alleged that Sanks King "failed in her job and failed the taxpayers of New Jersey who paid her salary. Not being charged with a crime is hardly an exoneration of that performance or a justification for continued employment" (Margolin 2009).

Bergen, appointed by Republican Governor Cahill. But, in the end, there were limits to Bergen's influence and it was another Republican governor who prevailed. During the tenure of Bergen's successor, Stuart Cook, presidential power was now limited and politically-based decision-makers directed the University's activities. That partisan politics played an overt role in how the University was run was made apparent by the resignation of Dr. Cook once Democratic Governor McGreevey was elected. McGreevey's appointment of Dr. Petillo allowed the presidential practice of engaging in the political world to continue. But that President's power would soon be curtailed by the Governor's resignation and the intercession of a Republican-appointed U.S. Attorney investigating the University's financial and other practices. The next president, William Owen Jr., appointed under Democratic Governor Corzine, would then operate with reduced power both internally and in the surrounding political environment. In the end, he too would succumb to the ambitions of an incoming governor of the opposing political party, now prepared to make extensive policy changes affecting the University.

School Administration

Each school within UMDNJ was headed by its own dean, also formally hired by the Board of Trustees, and each dean had the authority to hire associate and assistant deans who assumed administrative responsibilities. How these appointments were made varied over time, as was the role played by individual deans. The dean's office was typically the venue for handling the academic affairs of the school, coordinating the activities of individual departments, and ratifying decisions that emanated from them. Most detail is given about the history of the three medical schools because all of them played some role in the unfolding institutional corruption.

Since 1970, when the medical school inherited from Seton Hall officially became the New Jersey Medical School (NJMS), there had been nine deans. Three, including President Bergen, served in an acting capacity for, at most, two years and two others were considered interim, one for less than a year and the other, Robert L. Johnson, from 2005 until 2011, when his appointment was finally made permanent.

Robert Schwartz's (2005) fifty year history of medical education in the state suggests an inherent tension between the University president, by which he meant President Bergen, and the medical school dean, at least at NJMS. This tension can be surmised from the descriptors he attaches to several of the deans. The first of these, Rulon Dawson, who was in place when Dr. Bergen took over, is described as "vigorous." Harold Kaminetsky, who went from acting to formal capacity between 1972 and 1974, was "soothing." Vincent Lanzoni, the longest serving dean, whose term ran for 12 years beginning in 1975, was "more malleable." After another acting dean, Stuart Cook, who would later serve as acting and then formal president, stepped down, he was replaced by the "venerable" Ruy V. Lourenço. Dr. Lourenço came to NJMS from the University of Illinois Medical School, where he had been head of the Department of Medicine. His tenure of almost 11 years is described by Schwartz as leading to "renewed respect" for the medical school. Then, after another brief interim dean, Russell T. Joffe was hired.

Dr. Joffe, a "rising star" in medical education, is a native of South Africa, where he obtained his medical and psychiatric degrees. He had been a researcher and university professor at two universities in Canada, and a dean at one of them. Dr. Joffe's tenure as dean at NJMS lasted from 2001 until his resignation in 2005. No official reason was given for the resignation, although Dr. Joffe said that he wished to return to teaching. It is likely that at least two factors played a role in his resignation. One was a lack of popularity with his faculty, who criticized him for his management style (Stewart 2005d) and pressured the administration to remove him (Editorial 2005). Second was the accumulation of administrative and financial problems that had beset the University and his medical school in particular (Heyboer and Margolin 2005). It was suggested that he was encouraged to step down by President Petillo through the inducement of a "faculty renewal leave" even though he had not been employed the full six years the University required for receiving such an award (Stewart 2005e).

The last Dean, Robert L. Johnson, a graduate of UMDNJ and a faculty member in pediatrics, came to his position when UMDNJ was already under a cloud. In commenting on his possible appointment, the *Star-Ledger* Editorial (2005) said that "he has a reputation for speaking softly but taking no excuses. He comes with the advantage of knowing the medical school as a learner as well as a teacher and should be familiar with the often contentious in-house politics." When Dr. Johnson was appointed, Emanuel Goldman, president of the faculty association, described him as "very well-spoken and an intelligent consensus-builder who has earned the affection of many faculty" (Stewart 2005). Yet Dr. Johnson was kept in an interim appointment for six years and only given the position officially in 2011. During the time of his interim status, NJMS conducted two national searches for a dean while living through federal and state investigations and supervision by a federal monitor (Heyboer 2011).

Robert Wood Johnson Medical School (RJWMS) retained a separate identity with its own dean and administration. Its predecessor was Rutgers Medical School, begun under the deanship of DeWitt Stetten, Jr. Dismayed by his school's transformation into RWJMS as part of the then CMDNJ, Stetten immediately resigned (Stetten 1983). Since then there had been six deans. James W. McKenzie served from 1971 through 1975, followed by David J. Gocke. The tenure of Richard Reynolds, from 1979 to 1987, was one of augmented authority by virtue of his simultaneously holding the vice presidency for academic affairs. He was followed by Norman H. Edelman, who later left for SUNY at Stony Brook, where he served as Vice President for Health Sciences and Dean of the School of Medicine. Harold J. Paz was dean of RWJMS from 1995 until he resigned in 2006 to accept an administrative post at Penn State. Peter S. Amenta, the latest dean and a member of the medical school since 1989, served in an interim capacity for two years while a national search was underway.

Like the experiences of deans in NJMS, there were tensions between RWJMS deans and the central administration that, according to some participants, were even more contentious. It was said that "Dean Reynolds stuck it out as long as he could" while Dean Edelman's disputes with President Bergen led to the former being fired. In addition, RWJMS administrators and faculty felt their school was treated poorly in comparison with NJMS because of President Bergen's favoritism. Underlying these feelings was a residue of resentment left from the fissure with Rutgers University and a sense of comparative academic superiority. In response, NJMS saw RWJMS as elitist and over-identified with Rutgers.

The youngest of the three medical schools associated with UMDNJ, the School of Osteopathic Medicine, had, as its first dean, Benjamin Cohen. He was followed by two interim deans, each of whom served for one year. In 1986 Frederick Humphrey was appointed dean, a position he held until R. Michael Gallagher became dean in 2002. Chapter 2 described Dr. Gallagher's relations with State Senator Wayne Bryant, leading to criminal convictions for both. Dr. Gallagher was sentenced to eighteen months for bribery and fraud. Chapter 2 documented, as well, other problems in the Dean's office associated with his aide, Warren Wallace. On Dr. Gallagher's resignation, Thomas A. Cavaliere was appointed Dean on an interim basis. He served in that capacity for two years and received the position permanently in 2008. Although SOM had relied on RWJMS for some of the training received by its students, it was viewed with some disdain by both allopathic medical schools.

Of the remaining schools, the Dental School had also displayed behaviors that came under public scrutiny,[8] although some questions were raised about

---

8 In addition to problems with student exams and grading, reported in Chapter 2, it was found that Dr. Richard Montgomery had practiced dentistry at NJDS without a valid license (Stern 2008: 17–19).

the financial audits of the Nursing School's joint program in Guyana (Stern 2007). From its beginnings with Seton Hall, there have been ten deans in the Dental School. Three – Allan Formicola, Charles Vevier, and LeRoy A. Parker, Jr. – served briefly in an acting capacity. Three others, Richard Buchanan, Robert A. Saporito, and Cecile Feldman, began in an acting or interim role and continued as deans. Tenure for official deans ranged from one year to 11, the latter, at the time of writing, descriptive of the current dean, Cecile Feldman.

In the context of university administration generally, the role of dean can be a powerful one, shaping the goals of his/her school and the departments reporting to him/her. Even when deans head schools with quite different mandates, for example, medicine compared to journalism, there is always an element of competition over internal resources, including those of status. At UMDNJ, such competition was even more prevalent, given the existence of three medical schools, even though they were separated geographically and by the populations they served. Moreover, from the testimony of long-time faculty member Robert Schwartz (2005) about the tension between President Bergen and NJMS's deans, combined with reports from those familiar with RWJMS, there was continuity in the inherent conflict between the centralizing tendencies of the President's office and the search for autonomy by all deans. Among the indicators of this tension was the reliance on interim appointments, even when these were normally for less than two years. In the case of NJMS, a dean was allowed to remain in an acting capacity for six years before he received a final appointment. Even if that simply reflected the difficulty in attracting candidates during two external searches done in a period of turmoil, it still meant withholding full authority from that dean, Dr. Johnson.

Faculty and Staff

Faculty were hired on the basis of their formal qualifications–normally a Ph.D., M.D., or similar professional degree–and promoted through demonstration of increased skill and recognition within the appropriate scholarly community. Those attributes could be signaled by publications, success in obtaining grants, scientific advances, and contributions to the university community. Hiring, promotions, and salary recommendations were initiated by individual departments and schools, supported by faculty oversight committees, and then ratified by the administration in the relevant hierarchy before given final approval by the Board of Trustees. All these procedures were governed by University-wide bylaws and by more specific ones associated with each school, all of which had been formally approved by the Board of Trustees. Within departments, heads played a powerful role, augmented by their own high salaries and lengthy tenure,[9] through their ability to recommend rewards in salary. This latter flexibility was especially important for initial hires, when compensation could be a strong factor in bringing new talent to the department. Yet hiring for senior positions, even when associated with external searches, was reported by those interviewed to have buttressed an insular atmosphere that favored internal hires and discouraged broad searches.

Full-time academic faculty members were expected to participate in teaching, research, and provision of services appropriate to their School. There were also part-time faculty who performed the same activities but whose professional careers were partially fulfilled outside the University. Their titles reflected this status by the prefix "adjunct" – for example, adjunct associate professor. In addition, there were faculty who were primarily involved in patient care and they too could be full-time or part-time. These were identified by the prefix "clinical" – for example, clinical assistant professor. The designation of rank within the three categories of appointment was expected to follow the same University-wide criteria of mastery of subject matter, teaching effectiveness, scholarly productivity, and contributions to the service goals of the University.

One source for clinical appointments was physicians employed at hospitals that had a University affiliation. For the hospitals, such appointments provided a link with interns and residents who were graduates from UMDNJ as well as an opportunity to train graduates of other universities. For clinical faculty, appointments were opportunities to be involved in teaching and professional socialization. Clinical faculty could even be voluntary, in which case they were unpaid. For the latter, rewards were in status, not money. In addition, because physicians with large, independent practices could be an important source of referrals, the University began a strategy under President Bergen to purchase their practices and have the physicians become salaried employees of one of its hospitals (Whitlow 1995). But when this strategy was manipulated, as it was in the case of the eighteen cardiologists hired with no apparent duties except to funnel their patients to University Hospital, discussed in Chapter 2, federal laws were violated.

The example of the improperly hired cardiologists suggests how formal procedures, based on hiring and promoting faculty according to accepted standards of professional competence, could mesh with practices of patronage and cronyism that became formalized under President Petillo, also described in

9 These were among complaints by Dr. Steven Simring, who would be the principal whistleblower on Medicaid fraud (Carney 2008).

Chapter 2. It could have been possible for UMDNJ to have had two independent systems, with one where faculty was hired according to professional criteria and a second, where everyone else was subject, at least some of the time, to patronage considerations. That would have been relatively easy to institute because many staff positions entailed skills that were readily available. But, in fact, higher level positions, especially administrative ones, were too attractive to totally escape being coveted as vehicles of influence. For governors, in particular, such positions were ways of ensuring that their political agendas were incorporated into the University. This was exemplified by James Archibald, who moved from the Republican administration of Governor Whitman to become Senior Vice President of Administration and Finance under President Bergen. Knowledgeable faculty continued to identify the partisan affiliation of administrators as relevant to how they carried out their activities and to compare the political astuteness of faculty able to navigate the system. Moreover, the attractiveness of University employment not only meant that some politicians wanted jobs for themselves or their clients, but that senior administrators, eager to promote the interests of the University with the political establishment, would offer jobs to those they felt could be helpful. Examples included President Bergen hiring Steven Adubato, a Newark political figure, and, under President Petillo's administration, the hiring of State Senator Wayne Bryant at the same time as Bryant was chairman of the Senate Budget and Appropriations Committee. The porous boundaries between the University and its political milieu were an invitation to institutional corruption, a consequence of the competitive environment in which the University operated, where administrators could bend rules in order to build up the position of the University itself.

Relations within the Core

Hierarchical Relations

Relations within the core of UMDNJ can be described either hierarchically, from the administration downward, or laterally, across schools and departments. I begin with hierarchical relations, focusing on those participants described as contentious in the expectation that they will be more likely linked to the corrupting potential in hierarchy.

Relations between the administration and faculty and staff were both direct and mediated through external organizations that enabled different components of the UMDNJ work staff to improve and protect their working conditions through organizing and collective bargaining. To be fully consistent with the scheme outlined at the outset of this chapter, those organizations belong with the network described in Chapter 5. But because they were so much a part of the ongoing experiences of faculty and staff in navigating the prevailing hierarchical relations, they deserve treatment as part of the core.

The American Association of University Professors (AAUP) was the official negotiating agent for faculty and librarians with at least 50 percent appointments. Excluded were all managerial categories as well as faculty and program directors in the School of Health Related Professions – the latter were represented by the New Jersey Education Association. The university affiliate of AAUP was called the Council of Chapters in recognition of its division into two chapters. One was made up of NJMS, the Dental and Nursing Schools, the Graduate School of Biomedical Sciences, and the libraries. The second covered RWJMS and the Schools of Osteopathic Medicine and Public Health. Contention between AAUP and the university administration centered on contract negotiations and allegations that faculty terminations were made without due process (AAUP-UMDNJ).

Physicians who were interns and residents and worked at the thirteen UMDNJ-affiliated hospitals were represented by the Committee of Interns and Residents (CIR). CIR acted as a collective bargaining unit in negotiating contracts over issues like salaries, work hours, parking fees, maternity leave, and holidays. Those negotiations were with the university's central administration, not individual hospitals, and had a history of contention (e.g. *Star-Ledger* 1990a).

Hospital-employed registered nurses voted to unionize in 1990, joining the Hospital Professionals and Allied Employees of New Jersey (HPAE), an affiliate of the American Federation of Teachers. The movement to unionize was fought over a two year period and led to accusations that the university administration had led a concerted anti-union campaign (*Star-Ledger* 1990b). In 1992 nurses were followed into the HPAE by non-supervisory professional employees. Their unit included research teaching specialists, medical technologists, pharmacists, social workers, counselors, mental health clinicians and respiratory therapists (*Star-Ledger* 1992). In 2003 nurses at University Hospital voted to authorize a strike over issues of wages and staff ratios to patients (Stewart 2003b). They were soon joined by professional staff, who authorized a strike shortly after, dissatisfied at the way salary was tied to seniority (*Star-Ledger* 2003b).

Non-professional employees were organized in a number of different bargaining units. The Communication Workers of America, Local 1031, was part of the union's Public, Healthcare and Education Workers Sector and covered all university first-line supervisors except those in nursing, police, and EMS.

The local had been involved in difficult contract negotiations, precipitated by the furloughing of employees especially at University Hospital (CWA 1031). The president of local 1031 since 2003, John E. Rose, had been demoted for his union activities in 1997 but, on appeal, he was reinstated in 2000.

Police officers and sergeants each had their own lodge within the Fraternal Order of Police while security officers and public safety dispatchers were represented by the Office and Professionals International Union. Skilled trades were organized by the International Union of Operating Engineers. Emergency staff was divided between the International Association of EMTS and Paramedics, covering EMS supervisors, and the Teamsters, covering paraprofessional service staff of LPNS, EMTS, and paramedics.

Alongside contractual agreements on salary, working conditions, promotions, and termination were areas of discretion, available to administrators in handing out individual rewards and punishments. Reference has already been made to some of these practices in Chapter 2. On the reward side, perhaps most important was the flexibility to add to the base salary through patient care and faculty practice income. Discretion was also reflected in the ability to hire 18 cardiologists as feeders into the cardiology program at NJMS and University Hospital. Another sign of discretion was a severance policy that gave "golden parachutes" to administrators leaving UMDNJ even when, as in the case of James Archibald, they were alleged to have been involved in questionable activities (Sherman and Margolin 2005). Severance packages included two years of salary and, in some cases, health insurance, cars, office space and clerical assistance, cellular phones, computers, and job-search assistance (State Commission of Investigation 2007:66). Administrators also had access to generous bonuses in addition to salaries and seemingly unlimited travel expenses (Stern 2006a). For example, in 2005, $3.2 million in bonuses were scheduled for payment to 200 executives and managers, including $187,000 to President Petillo (Carney 2005). Dean R. Michael Gallagher of the School of Osteopathic Medicine used his additional position as Chair of the Headache Center to fraudulently obtain bonuses (US District Court of NJ 2006).

Although there were statutory and contractual constraints on punishments that administrators could use against employees, administrators were also able to rely on their discretionary powers to punish those who challenged the authority structure. Criticism of financial practices in the University or its hospitals was the prime reason for withdrawing benefits and terminating employment. Although redress was sought through the courts, results were generally not in favor of the plaintiff. Examples suggest that the ability to silence opposition was closely linked to the University's ability to continue along troubling paths.

An early sign of how complaints were handled administratively appeared in the case of Norma Davenport, an attorney for the University. She was suspended in October, 1986 after eight years of employment and terminated in September 1988. In arguing against her ouster, Davenport filed a 30-count complaint that foreshadowed future charges. It included "violations of public bidding laws in real estate ventures, conflicts of interest among the faculty, use of public funds to pay for malpractice insurance covering doctors' private work, and corruption within an ambulance service and abortion clinic" (Curcio 1989). The lawsuit was filed with the New Jersey Superior Court in Newark by her attorney, Michael Critchley, who alleged that the university violated the Racketeering Influenced Corrupt Organizations (RICO) act. Among those charged were President Bergen; Herbert Roemmele, chairman of the Board of Trustees; board members Dr. Michael Bernstein, Dr. Franklyn Gerard, and Jerome Pollack; senior Vice President for Administration Paul Gazzero; and senior Vice President for Academic Affairs and Dean of RWJMS Dr. Richard Reynolds. These charges were an extension of more personal ones filed against the university two years previously. The court rejected the suit, stating it was not filed on time.

Other cases reveal the unstable tension between the University's discretion in allocating rewards and punishments. Administrators could offer inducements to those with the potential to bring desirable resources to the University and then withdraw them when those receiving those resources appeared to challenge administrative authority. One example stems from offers to Paul Larson to motivate his move to UMDNJ as Senior Vice President for Academic Affairs. Among them was a sizable loan to make a home purchase, a loan that Larson interpreted as part of his benefit package. But once he was fired after 9 years at the University, the University argued that Larson owed it more than $600,000. In his counter-charges, Larson argued that he had been misled about the terms of the loan. More critically, the university was said to lack the authority to even make such loans (Quinn 1998).

A second illustration of the tensions between the administration's efforts to recruit top flight faculty and its reaction to challenges, once faculty were in place, is provided by Dr. David M. Goldenberg. Goldenberg, a recognized authority in the field of biological medical strategies, had been recruited in 1983 to start the university's cancer center on a scope comparable to Memorial Sloan-Kettering Cancer Center or Dana-Farber Cancer Institute. The new center was established as the Center for Molecular Medicine and Immunology (CMMI), a private, non-profit entity housed at UMDNJ's Newark campus. CMMI paid rent for its facilities to the University but soon found them inadequate. Fueled by this and other complaints, Dr. Goldenberg began building a program in Belleville (MacPherson 1995). To this point, his scientific achievements had been recognized by the National Cancer Institute, which renewed a $7 to $11 million grant over seven years. But driven by uneasiness that an independent operation would come to compete with the University, UMDNJ proceeded to create its own Cancer Institute of New Jersey as part of RWJMS, supported by a planning grant from the National Cancer Institute. Meanwhile, Dr. Goldenberg's clinical arrangements with the University were dissolved in 1992. Still, his departure was not quick enough for the University and it filed a suit against him in 1995 to evict him from his office and research space (Fisher 1998). But in the Essex County Superior Court hearing, the Court ruled in Dr. Goldenberg's favor, finding that the University did not have grounds to evict him and it would jeopardize his research if he left before his new facility was available (Schwab 1995).

A third instance involved the Dental School and the autonomy of a research center (Dental Research Center/DRC) that had been set up in 1985 by then Dean Dr. LeRoy Parker and Dr. Francis Shovlin, with assurances that the Center's director would have full authority to run it. But administrative changes within the Dental School and the appointment of Dr. Paul Larson as Senior Vice President for Academic Affairs brought about efforts for greater administrative control over DRC. These resulted in legal challenges by Dr. Shovlin over what he saw as violations of the original contractual understandings about the director's authority and concerns over the direction of DRC (Shovlin v. University of Medicine and Dentistry 1998).

Discretionary sanctioning ability was not, as these and other cases illustrate, entirely without limits, even though redress relied on costly appeals to external authority. The protections of faculty tenure could prevail even in the most contentious relations, exemplified by the case of Dr. Sanford Klein, chief of anesthesia services at RWJ Hospital and chairman of the anesthesiology department at RWJMS, when he was removed from the chairmanship in 1999. He had been a faculty member for 16 years and still had four years in his contract as chairman. In his suit against RWJMS and its hospital; UMDNJ; RWJ Healthcare Corporation (the billing agency for physicians); the hospital president, Harvey Holzberg; and the medical school dean, Harold Paz, Dr Klein alleged he had been punished as a result of his complaints about relations with billing agencies and conflicts of interest. The substance of his complaint was twofold. In 1997 Dr. Klein had negotiated a settlement with U.S. Healthcare, an HMO, over late payments, but Dr. Paz, who had served as a consultant for U.S. Healthcare, abandoned the settlement and allowed it to escape its outstanding debts. Then, in 1999, Dr. Holzberg allowed the acute care facility in Hamilton to drop its contract with the Anesthesia Services group, an organization of the medical school's anesthesiologists, to both the benefit of the hospital and of increased compensation for Dr. Holzberg (Tyrrell 2000).[10] Although punishments did not deter Dr. Klein from continued complaints, now directed against safety conditions in the Radiology Department (Sanford L. Klein, D.D.S., M.D. v. University of Medicine and Dentistry 2005), the University was upheld in eliminating Dr. Klein's faculty practice component of salary in 2004 (Public Employment Relations Commission 2009).

Charges related to overbilling were an especially critical arena for conflict, where those who complained were forced into silence. Among those affected was Karen Silliter, then chief compliance officer, who had noticed that the computer system was configured to charge the maximum reimbursement rate for all Medicare patients. When she reported this to her superiors, she was told to redraft her report. Seven months later, she was forced to resign (Margolin and Sherman 2005a) Adam Henick, vice president for ambulatory care at University Hospital, said that, when he became aware of double billing, he informed his superiors who formed a task force to investigate. Frustrated by the pace of the task force, he threatened to inform federal investigators. Henick was then kept from knowing when task force meetings were held and eventually fired (Moran 2005). James Lawler was chief financial officer at University Hospital and, according to Henick, one of those informed of overbilling in 2002. Although Lawler appeared to respond appropriately to this information, it was not until 2005 that he would refuse to sign federal documents certifying to the accuracy of Medicare and Medicaid bills (Margolin and Sherman 2005a). He resigned shortly after, claiming that he been subject to coercion to sign and, on his refusal, forced to resign (Williams 2007). At least four other cases involved people who complained about irregularities in billing and were subsequently fired (Margolin and Sherman 2007). Even while under federal oversight, the University continued to overbill and complaints by the chief financial officer of University Hospital, Edward Burke, led to his termination (Friedman 2008).

The case of the improperly hired cardiologists provided another arena for conflict between faculty and administrators. These local physicians, although contractually required to perform a range of clinical duties, were, in fact, hired primarily to recommend patients to University Hospital despite the illegality of that action (Stern 2006c). The major internal complainant about the hiring

10 Tyrrell (2000) describes Dr. Klein's punishments as though he had been fired from the hospital and University. In fact, Klein remained as a faculty member until the time of writing, though no longer as chairman. His hospital privileges were limited and he lost the ability to benefit from the physicians' practice plan.

was Dr. Rohit Arora, then chief of the Division of Cardiology. Dr. Arora, who was serving without tenure, was then forced to resign. Without admitting wrongdoing, the University paid Dr. Arora $2.2 million to settle his wrongful termination suit (Margolin and Sherman 2006a, b). With Bruce Vladeck now serving as interim President, and denying any knowledge of wrongdoing (Stern 2006c: 24–25), the University shifted blame by placing two officials on administrative leave. One was Dr. Jerome Ellner, chairman of the Department of Medicine at NJMS, and the other, Ronald Pittore, who had taken over management of the legal department after the firing of its head, Sanks King, for what was seen as her ineffectiveness in handling the billing issues (Margolin and Sherman 2006c).

Although administrative control was tight and rewards and punishments were relatively effective in keeping faculty and staff in line, they were far from perfect and individuals challenged them, with varying degrees of success. A graphic demonstration of the ambiguity surrounding administrative practices and judgments about their propriety comes from the experiences of Warren Wallace of the School of Osteopathic Medicine. Wallace had been fired as a result of the federal monitor raising questions about his simultaneous duties as Gloucester County Freeholder, his handling of petty cash and a no-bid contract, and his efforts to obtain admission to SOM for his daughter (Stern 2006b). Wallace (2008) vigorously defended his actions and complained that no one would give him a direct hearing. He filed suit against wrongful termination, charging racial discrimination, and received a settlement of $60,000 (Hefler 2010).

The individual who benefitted most from becoming a whistleblower was Dr. Steven S. Simring, who had been an associate professor of psychiatry at NJMS. A year before criminal charges were filed against the University for double-billing Medicare and Medicaid, Dr. Simring had brought a complaint to the U.S. Attorney. When the University paid the federal government a fine of $2 million, Simring was rewarded with over $800,000 (Santiago 2009).

I conclude from this review that hierarchical relations in the core organization dominated within all units. That is, power resided in the top administration and provided the model followed by those running individual schools and departments. For university-wide administrators, in particular, control was aided by the discretionary use of rewards and punishments. Outside the specific guarantees to employment conditions that were ensured through collective bargaining, it was difficult to challenge administrative authority.[11]

11 The most far-reaching vindication against administrative practices came in 2012, when forty years of discrimination against women faculty with respect to salaries was finally redressed by a settlement of $4.6 million (Alex 2012c).

Lateral Relations

Relations within all U.S. universities, their schools and departments, even though hierarchical in nature, have an important lateral component arising from the collegial nature of professional and university responsibilities. A sense of shared identity and values is expected to extend beyond the boundaries of individual departments and to encompass the university as a community of scholars. Among the major ways through which universities work to achieve that ideal are mentoring, scholarly collaboration, and self-governance.

UMDNJ's approach to mentoring was based on the view, expressed by President Stuart Cook at his inauguration in 1999, that great teachers could be a life-long inspiration to their students. This led to the establishment of a Master Educators' Guild, to which faculty could be recommended by their deans and then ratified by a University-wide committee. Membership came with a title, medallion, and unrestricted funds for furthering scholarly activities. Guild members soon recognized that, whatever mentoring was done, occurred informally, at the discretion of individual departments. Their recommendations, formally approved in 2004, proposed that

> UMDNJ and its schools establish formal mentoring procedures for both junior and senior faculty. For junior faculty, the goal should be to help develop them into successful, mature faculty. For the senior faculty, the goal should be to maintain and enhance their productivity and effectiveness as scientists, educators, administrators and/or clinicians.
>
> UMDNJ MASTER EDUCATORS' GUILD 2004

Under the aegis of administrative units dealing with research programs in each of the schools, faculty mentoring programs were then set up to guide junior faculty in pursuing their professional careers. In the period leading up to the appointment of the federal monitor, however, mentoring appears to have been more a matter of happenstance, depending on the inclinations of individuals, rather than a concerted University policy.

Collaborative activities are a second means by which colleagueship can be fostered. It may occur through joint teaching or research among faculty of the same or different rank, and within or across departments, schools, or universities. Unlike in the humanities and, to a lesser extent, the social sciences, where the norm is for research and publications to be the work of a sole researcher, the sciences, including medicine, are much more likely to involve multiple researchers. The latter may work in the same lab or they may draw on skills and resources from diverse settings. But when collaboration crosses boundaries, whether of disciplines or physical locations, it raises questions about who will receive the largest share of credit when assessing contributions, making it necessary to negotiate how recognition is shared. In medical schools, as in science departments, where large investments are made in laboratories and equipment, senior faculty may have their names on published papers even when they have done no more than provide approval for using facilities. Overall, the multiple campuses and three medical schools were reported by participants to have discouraged collaborative research that breached their boundaries.

Over the years, multiple research centers and institutes were set up to enhance scholarly output and visibility for the University (UMDNJ Research website). They could do this by facilitating research for all schools within UMDNJ, as was the case for the Clinical Research Organization, which offered incentives in the form of information that could link industries with university researchers in undertaking clinical trials. They could be a laboratory setting for conducting research and training students, as was the case for the Neurological Institute of New Jersey, a joint venture of the three medical schools. Such settings could be confined to a single school, most commonly descriptive of centers associated with RWJMS, like the Child Health or the Cancer Institutes of New Jersey, with the latter also involved in patient treatment. RWJMS also had collaborative relations with Rutgers University in the Center for Advanced Biotechnology and Medicine and in the Environmental and Occupational Health Sciences Institute. Some centers focused on patient treatment and outreach to the community, like the Limb Lengthening and Deformity Correction Center at NJMS or the University Craniofacial Center of New Jersey, a joint undertaking of NJMS and the Dental School. In total, although these centers and institutes provided numerous avenues for encouraging collaborative activities, when those did occur, it was almost always within the confines of individual schools.

Finally, a sense of community can be encouraged through institutions of shared governance. Such institutions provide forums in which faculty, at different stages in their careers and with different interests and commitments, can come together to engage in meaningful debate that allows the possibility of influencing decisions and altering the status quo. Such institutions could, ideally, be found at all organizational levels, from the individual department to the central administration.

The primary vehicle for faculty participation and input is normally a senate, made up of members elected from the faculty (often excluding administrators) and concerned with the totality of issues affecting the university. For example, although setting a budget is normally the responsibility of the administration, the senate may attempt to influence that document through its judgments about the amount and allocation of revenues. In the case of UMDNJ, the senate was perceived as an ineffectual body and abolished in 2005 (Richardson and Martinez 2009: 210). Only in 2011 was it reestablished as an elected, university-wide body. To ensure that it would represent faculty concerns, it excluded all administrative personnel, whether department chairs, anyone with "dean" in his or her title, or any member of the central administration.

Without a viable senate as a vehicle for faculty representation and an arena for even modest countervailing power to the administration, shared governance was confined to the administrative structures and practices recognized in each school's bylaws (e.g., New Jersey Dental School 2005). Whether concerned with the governance of an individual department, research center or institute, or entire school, these bodies were always headed by the administrative officer in charge of the unit. Although units could vary by their openness to rank and file influence, depending on the proclivities of their heads, their histories, and the nature of their composition, virtually all of them would still be constrained by their structure.

None of this means that faculty influence was necessarily negligible, only that it lacked one of the avenues traditionally available in universities. To the extent that faculty well-being was ensured, it was through the efforts of the unions that bargained for it with the administration. Yet however effective that bargaining might be in promoting both faculty and staff interests and protecting their employment rights, it was relatively weak in enhancing the University as a community of scholars. This particular weakness was anticipated earlier, where I described organizing and collective bargaining institutions as an important component of the hierarchical relations characterizing the organizational core. For the most part, building a sense of community and the colleagueship that goes with it had to rely mainly on informal bonds, whatever mentoring existed, and the opportunities for collaboration inherent in the University's array of research centers and institutes.

Vulnerability in the Core

This description of UMDNJ lays out the complexity of its core organization along with evidence of how that complexity evolved and increased over time. In summarizing its most prominent features, I do so to highlight how these made UMDNJ vulnerable to its ensuing corruption.

Hierarchy

One overriding characteristic of UMDNJ was its hierarchical organization, emanating from the office of President and repeated at every level in all its units. Such hierarchies are common to all modern bureaucracies and are one means used to promote adherence to uniform standards with accompanying efficiencies in outputs (Magee and Galinsky 2008). Among the factors making hierarchy an effective organizational tool are a consistent and unbroken chain of command, the free flow of information, and the acknowledgment of legitimacy to those who exercise authority. In itself, the hierarchy associated with bureaucratic organization is nominally neutral with respect to its ethical or legal operation. At the same time, the three characteristics I identify as contributing to hierarchy's effectiveness can also be the source of potentially deleterious effects,[12] as appeared to be the case for UMDNJ.

The model of a strong president running a centralized organization was set by President Bergen. It would then become part of UMDNJ's organizational culture, shaping how every administrative officer was expected to perform. At the same time, an element of inconsistency was introduced through the discretionary ability of top administrators to offer rewards and punishments. And no matter how well deans and department chairs were able to exercise their own authority, it was virtually inevitable that some would chafe at constraints imposed by those higher in the administrative chain and would then seek to side step them.

After Dr. Bergen's retirement, President Cook, weakened by his initial status as acting president and, as an internal candidate, unable to exert the same control as his predecessor, left a power vacuum that was filled by overtly political aides. President Petillo may have aspired to strength comparable to Dr. Bergen's, demonstrated by the former's efforts to ensure ties with the external political milieu. But the kind of overt politicization associated with those efforts conveyed a message inconsistent with the academic goals of the University. If Bruce Vladek might have been a different kind of strong president, he was given little opportunity to demonstrate this and his replacement by President Owen ensured that there would be less centralized control. With hindsight from knowledge of the abuses that occurred over the course of these presidencies, it would appear that vulnerability to corruption could arise under either strong or weak presidents. A strong presidency may have been the core model, but it had lost much of its potency even before Dr. Bergen's departure and its potential as a restraining factor against corruption was never realized.

---

12 Hamel (2011) gives a sardonic overview of the strengths and weaknesses of hierarchical organization.

An effective hierarchy depends on the free flow of information. To those lower in the chain, it informs them of issues and of appropriate responses. Information flowing to those higher in the chain supplies measures of productivity and alerts them to problems. This kind of information exchange is an important component of transparency and hence an ingredient in forestalling corruption. Many of the troubling incidents discussed in this and Chapter 2, for example, those related to billing procedures, the avoidance of contracts, and cronyism in hiring or agreements with vendors, all depended on deliberately constructed barriers to the exchange of information. Other barriers, whether intended or not, existed because of the geographic dispersion of campuses and the even more widespread distribution of affiliated centers and hospitals. That dispersion led to a kind of loose coupling that contributed to the fostering of local interests (Scott and Davis 2007). Further barriers could arise from competition for resources among units. Given the various ways in which information flows could be impeded, the potential for corruption was consequently enhanced.

In organizational settings, claims for legitimacy are based on recognized qualifications for the occupancy of positions of authority. Even though it is the office rather than the individual office-holder that bears the claims to legitimacy, both may come to enjoy expressions of deference. I separate deference from legitimacy because, while the latter is associated with compliant acceptance, the former implies expressions of esteem and even submissiveness. Authority can be accepted while still being open to disagreements; deference leaves no room for questioning. Deference enters relations through attitudes cultivated by the profession of medicine as it dominates all health-related fields, a condition endemic in UMDNJ by the very fact that, as a university, it was focused exclusively on health care. Because such deferential relations reinforce the acceptance of hierarchy and a reluctance to question authority, they promote an organizational culture that, under the right circumstances, can lead to practices unchecked by scrutiny or challenge.[13] It is then that deviance may emerge.

Dependence

Equally prominent was UMDNJ's dependent character. Its dependence on resources, both for normal day to day operations and for new ventures, ensured that the University would exist in a constant state of uncertainty about their sources, continuity, and magnitude (Pfeffer and Salancik 1978). For the most

13 It is such a "culture of unquestioning obedience to leadership" that Dunn and Schweitzer (2005: 52) link to unethical behavior.

part, resources existed outside the core and shaped relations between the core and its network, discussed in the following chapter. In addition, within the organizational core, uncertainty was the norm with respect to revenues for providing services, particularly patient care at University Hospital but also elsewhere. As a consequence, the extent to which hospitals and clinical services would be a drain on University operations was often in question. For example, at the end of the 1996 academic year, 53 faculty members did not have their contracts renewed, almost all of whom were physicians caring for patients at University Hospital in Newark (Scott 1996). More generally, resource uncertainty meant that each year brought with it an inability to reliably estimate forthcoming resources, whether these involved money from the state, grants and contracts, or various measures of status. Uncertainty then led to openness to alternative solutions even if they were of dubious legality or fairness.

Organizations typically respond to uncertainty by adopting strategies of bridging or buffering (Scott and Davis 2007). Building and increasing stable bridges to the environment are ways to protect the core organization's power and reduce its dependency. Buffering strategies are aimed at protecting unique aspects of the core from external competition or control. Normally, one looks for such strategies in relation to the environment but there can also be some analogy to relations within the core. One arena in which these could be found are in the relations between schools and the higher administration or between departments and the deans of their schools.

Although UMDNJ's hierarchical structure would appear to impede independent strategies, in fact, there was some leeway for schools or departments to establish their own bridging efforts. They could do this by cultivating special relations with administrators and demonstrating their loyalty to them. In this regard, the physical proximity between NJMS and the central administration in Newark was viewed by those at RWJMS in New Brunswick as an avenue for the former to obtain greater access to resources. In effect, the use of such bridging techniques to obtain internal advantage in ways experienced as unfair to other schools or departments were then conducive to institutional corruption.

Schools and departments could also engage in buffering-like strategies. Conditions were set by the history of each school's origins, which lived on to mark its identity and embed it in its own network of relations. The result diminished any overall sense of common purpose and helped foster internal competition. Although such localized responses, akin to buffering strategies, need not, in themselves, have been corrupt, they were among the incentives to protect a unit's position in comparison to others. Buffering also enhanced a unit's control over information and helped in creating structural holes, which, in turn, could open opportunities for deviance.

Paths to Corruption

This overview of the history and organization of UMDNJ uncovered two major sources of weakness that made it vulnerable to engaging in illegal and unethical behavior, one in its hierarchical structure and the other in its resource dependency. Both dependency and defects in how hierarchy operated fostered incentives for deviant action and opened opportunities to do so. These outcomes can now be assessed more generally, according to how they conformed to the principal routes to corruption hypothesized in the previous chapter.

Buffeted by changes in higher education that were augmented by those specific to health-related fields, and by changing relations with all levels of government, UMDNJ's responses led to the emergence of competing norms and structures. Within its core, changes affected the training of students, patient care, faculty roles, and administrative responsibilities. They resulted in pitting faculty desires for autonomy against administrative control, professional values of service against administrative values of efficiency, and, expanding beyond the core, governmental demands for accountability against university independence. Each competitive milieu opened opportunities for potentially deviant responses by calling into question what, under less turmoil, could have been reasonably unambiguous demands. For example, since a medical resident already possesses a professional degree, the constraints that the federal government imposed on his/her unsupervised performance of a medical procedure could be dismissed by the university as an unnecessary administrative detail. Similarly, nurses' complaints about the limited time they were given for patient supervision and the oversight of students could be dismissed by administrators searching for ways to impose greater efficiencies. The results were invitations for illegitimate actions.[14] From these and other examples we can align the conflicting norms within UMDNJ's core organization with the expectations of H_1 that such conflicts open opportunities for corruption.

Most of the resources on which the University depended originated outside its core and were always subject to uncertainty. In addition, the demand for resources was always expanding. Incentives were consequently strong to both ensure access to increased resources and to establish avenues for banking resources outside the supervision of state authorities. The strength of

14 Although concerned with competition and conflict rather than uncovering opportunities for corruption, Scott (2004) finds comparable tensions among arguments for professional, state, or market-based dominance in the health care field.

those incentives could then, as predicted in H_2, lead to corrupt ways of behaving.

Although it is more appropriate to speak of embedded relations when dealing with UMDNJ's network relations, there were also aspects of embeddedness that affected the core. As an outgrowth of their embeddedness in the political world, along with the authority they had from their position in the university hierarchy, administrators had discretionary powers they could exercise, whether out of self-interest or in the interests they interpreted to be due the University. Whenever that discretion was exercised in ways seen as unfair, as it was with punishments used against those who complained or for rewards to administrators or favored faculty, it fulfilled the expectations of H_3.

The pressure to ensure adequate resources occurred within a competitive environment that both put administrators' jobs at risk and threatened the academic viability of the University. That exposure led to activities, such as overbilling in the hospitals, illegal hiring of cardiologists, and succumbing to political pressures, which were either knowingly directed by administrators or implicitly encouraged by them. As hypothesized in H_4, those who had responsibility for running UMDNJ also had responsibility for fostering an organizational culture that encouraged illegal and unethical behavior.

The hierarchical structure of UMDNJ, along with the variety and complexity of the tasks performed within its core, augmented conditions in which information flows were impeded and information itself was lacking in transparency. As one department chair observed, "We often wondered about how the billing office operated but no one could penetrate how decisions were made." The relation between lack of transparency and corruption supports H_5.

The origins of UMDNJ left their imprint on subsequent relations among schools, fostering long-held grievances. Along with internal competition for resources and the geographic dispersion of schools and research centers, these factors contributed to the absence of an encompassing collective identity. Internal rivalry then became an incentive to find advantages that benefitted particular segments of the University even when they involved illegal or unethical behavior, as anticipated in H_6.

The magnitude and complexity of information that could be exchanged within the organizational core went along with barriers to its free flow, augmented by the rise of structural holes. When administrative roles are separated from faculty ones in a setting of structural holes, opportunities for misconduct may go unchecked, as predicted in H_7.

The effects of structural holes were augmented due to an organizational culture that developed as a result of the dominance accorded medical professionals. That culture created a deferential atmosphere in which questioning authority was discouraged. H_9 expected that it would be in just such a setting that corruption could take hold.

Although the history and organization of UMDNJ may not have led it on an inevitable path to corruption, this assessment makes it clear that they supplied enough incentives and opportunities to transform it into a highly vulnerable setting, where slippage into corruption became relatively easy. They did so in ways congruent with processes known to lead to organizational corruption in general by supporting all the relevant hypothesized relations presented in Chapter 3. Chapter 5 now goes on to describe how those incentives and opportunities for misconduct multiplied when UMDNJ is viewed from the perspective of its interaction with others in its network.

CHAPTER 5

UMDNJ's Network Organization

The Network Defined

Captured only by its label, UMDNJ would be an incomplete organization. It cannot be understood in isolation from other bodies with which it interacted on a regular basis, often in ways that blurred the boundaries of the University itself. Primary among these were the New Jersey state government, whose actions enabled the University to exist and expand, or, demonstrated by its 2012 legislation, cease to do so. The government's most critical functions were divided between the Governor and the legislature and enabled it to make decisive appointments and supply basic funding. I give separate treatment to state government-sponsored agencies whose job it was to oversee the operation of the University. With the focus on New Jersey, the federal government's role in oversight is also reviewed. A third set of interacting bodies was concerned with accrediting the University and its component parts, enabling them to perform their activities with the legitimacy needed to serve students and patients. Since the process of accreditation is aimed at building the authority of practitioners, it was also linked to the professional identity and commitment of faculty. Another category of linked actors conferred status. These included funding agencies distinct from the legislature and organizations that publically ranked UMDNJ among its peers. The final category is that of community, which subsumes citizens groups, local political interests, service providers, other state and private institutions of higher education, and unaffiliated and competing hospitals.

UMDNJ, as the core organization described in the previous chapter, becomes an even more complex organization when embedded in a network of relations with others. Those relations are mediated by the resources in play, those who hold them, and how they are used. Resources consist of money, power, and status and may originate and be dominated by either the core or other network actors; their use may remain one-sided or become reciprocal.

Because resources vary in magnitude and in the certainty of access to them, this can lead them to become strong incentives to adopt illegal or unethical approaches to ensure their consistent flow to the University. At the same time, we should expect powerful constraints, stemming from moral and ethical standards or from legal prohibitions and fears of discovery, to keep temptation from becoming overt action. But given the uncertainty associated with resource dependency, such constraints will be overwhelmed at times for some organizational participants. Primed by incentives, the latter become alert for opportunities to act. Chapter 3 suggested basically two avenues through which opportunities could arise, already demonstrated in the preceding chapter. The first arose from major changes affecting the training and regulation of health care professionals that led to the coexistence of competing norms and structures. The results opened alternative pathways to accomplish goals and alternative justifications for actions taken, some of which would be defined as illegitimate. The second avenue was the result of embeddedness, opening opportunities for discretionary behavior, the ability to block transparency, the emergence of structural holes, and the manipulation of signals.

Just as in the case of the core organization described in the previous chapter, this chapter's description of network relations can be assessed with respect to expectations laid out in Chapter 3. Taken together, the view of UMDNJ that emerges is generally descriptive of other institutions of health care education. Similarly, vulnerabilities uncovered are directly applicable to the situations of those institutions. The connection between the particulars of UMDNJ experiences and the broader problem of corruption in higher education is further elaborated in the concluding chapter.

New Jersey Government

The Governor

New Jersey is governed by a strong governor, the sole state-wide elected officer with authority to appoint all other state-wide officials (Richardson and Martinez 2009: 188) and this strength was reflected in the relations between governors and UMDNJ. Although UMDNJ was an organ of the state, it did not conform to the concept of a normal state agency, like the departments of health or corrections, yet there are indications that governors saw it in an analogous light. Most telling was the governor's ability to appoint the president even when candidates for that office were recruited and vetted by a search committee. Even though this did not mean that governors acted quixotically, without regard to relevant input, the ultimate decision was theirs, shaped by how UMDNJ fit into their policy goals. Gubernatorial power was especially evident in the appointments of Presidents Cook and Petillo and earlier, of President Bergen. Using his official authority, Governor Codey could appoint Dr Rodgers to temporarily fill the role of President and Governor Corzine, to appoint interim President Bruce Vladek. Equally important were governors' ability to find ways to end a president's term, employed against Presidents Bergen and Cook. Aside from the special circumstances that put President

Petillo under pressure to resign by the U.S. Attorney, he could not survive for long, once his sponsor, Governor McGreevey, resigned.[1]

The Governor's power to appoint members of the Board of Trustees further ensured his or her authority over how the University was run. The Senate President could recommend two members, as could the Speaker of the Legislative Assembly, and the remaining voting members were approved with the advice and consent of the State Senate, but the Governor had control over the great majority of trustee appointments and also designated the Board's chair.

Of all the ways the Governor had an impact on the University, none was greater than control over the budget. Although each school developed its own budget that then became part of a single document, prepared by the University's central administration to incorporate other costs, its fate was decided by the state. Only after executive review by the Office of Management and Budget of the State Treasury Department and by the Governor's Office was it recommended to the legislature for approval. There, the legislative power of the purse was exercised in the Senate Budget and Appropriations Committee and the Assembly Budget Committee, both of which could do markups and hold hearings. But, ultimately, it was up to the Governor to sign the budget into law.

The Governor's power extended beyond the ability to make formal appointment, manifested through the movement of persons who held executive appointments in his/her office into positions within or attached to the University. Most prominent of these was James Archibald, who went from the Whitman administration to become Senior Vice President for Administration and Finance. He was accompanied by two other Whitman appointees who became University vice presidents, John Ekerios and Louis Goetting. Clifton Lacy, who was commissioner of health and senior services in the McGreevey administration, followed that Governor's resignation with his own to then take over as president and chief executive officer of the Robert Wood Johnson University Hospital (Epstein 2004).

During the period of special concern to this work, some governors were more actively involved than others in the affairs of UMDNJ. Governors McGreevey and Whitman stood out for their impact, as did Governor Richard J. Codey, who, after being elevated from the Senate on McGreevey's resignation, served briefly until 2006. Although Governor Corzine, who was elected in the midst of the federal monitor's activities, began office with multiple opportunities to shape the governance of UMDNJ, he appears to have lost interest,

1 While campaigning for governor, Jon Corzine said that he would not have picked Petillo to head the university. Once he became governor, and without consulting with the trustees, he quickly removed Petillo (Chen 2006).

once his chosen successor to the presidency came under attack by the U.S. Attorney and then withdrew from consideration for a permanent appointment. There is no evidence that the last president, Dr Owen, was appointed because of the active involvement of Governor Corzine. But once Chris Christie moved from being U.S. Attorney to becoming Governor, there was little doubt that he would be vigorous in pursuing his own agenda to determine the fate of UMDNJ.

State Legislature

Some of the Governor's authority over the University's budget and the appointment of trustees was constitutionally shared with the legislature. In both of these arenas, the legislature wielded considerable power by virtue of two interacting attributes. The first, and probably the most critical, was its representative nature, ensuring that local interests would have a voice in its decisions. The larger size of the Assembly served, in effect, to raise its members' volume. The second was the ability of both Houses to scrutinize and modify the budget through their openness to outside interests.

Evidence of legislative power over matters of budget and appointments has already been presented in Chapter 2. There the emphasis was not on how the legislature supported the University's normal operations but on how interactions between individual legislators and UMDNJ had become corrupted. In those cases, money for specific schools and programs was weighed with respect to how it would benefit local political interests, specific constituents, or legislators themselves. Recommendations for the appointment of University trustees were based on personal and local ties with legislators. Constituents and family members could benefit as well from those legislators' recommendations for University employment.

Because legislators could affect how funding was channeled to the University and its components, University officials made efforts to forge a direct line to this source of money. Dean Gallagher of the School of Osteopathic Medicine hired State Senator Wayne Bryant when the latter chaired the budget committee, resulting in a considerable inflation of SOM's income.[2] The benefits that came from having a legislator on the University payroll were also recognized by other organizations. They led John P. Ferguson, both a University trustee and director and CEO of Hackensack University Medical Center, affiliated with NJMS, to hire State Senator Joseph Coniglio for a part-time public relations job. Coniglio, a retired plumber, was a member of the State Senate Budget and

2 Those benefits would ultimately contribute to both parties' prison sentences, discussed in Chapter 2.

Appropriations Committee and successfully steered more than one million in state money to the hospital.[3]

The University reciprocated legislative relations by engaging in broader lobbying activities, intended to influence both state and federal governments. Under the Bergen and Petillo administrations, lobbyists were hired without soliciting bids and they were used to gain access to the governor as well as relevant legislative committees (Margolin 2005a; Margolin and McNichol 2005). They were employed, as well, to counter partisan criticisms of the University and to engage in election campaign activities (State Commission of Investigation 2007: 54–56).

Government Influence

Compared to other public universities in New Jersey, UMDNJ was considered to be under greater state supervision (McGuiness 1995: 3), which, in practice, served to emphasize the political nature of that supervision. Both the Governor and the legislature directly influenced UMDNJ's core organization through their control over resources of power and money. Of the two, the Governor's power appeared stronger; the legislature's ability to shape where money was directed may have given it a slight edge in control over that resource. Reciprocal impact from the University core, in particular, from its top administration, appeared to be relatively limited with respect to the Governor. It had greater scope to influence the legislature through resources of money and status. Money could be awarded to legislators in the form of salary or campaign contributions. Legislators could gain status whenever the University showed deference to them over their job recommendations. More tangible status came from the prestige of holding a paid position associated with the University. But use of resources in this manner was, at the least, morally ambiguous and easily slid into corruption.

State Oversight Agencies[4]

Commission on Higher Education

In the 1960s, New Jersey had a highly centralized system for regulating public higher education under a cabinet-level Department of Higher Education

3 As a result of his actions, Coniglio was convicted on six counts of fraud and extortion (Sherman 2009) and Ferguson's days were then numbered (*The Record* 2009).

4 Omitted from this discussion are the Presidents' Council, an advisory group for the Commission on Higher Education, and the Higher Education Student Assistance Authority, since neither was germane to this analysis of UMDNJ.

(DHE). The Department was administered by a chancellor and directed by a statewide Board of Higher Education (BHE). But pressure grew to give greater autonomy, particularly to the nine institutions considered "senior." During the 1980s, NJ had pursued improvements in higher education aided by the state's strong economy. These led to recognition of "New Jersey as one of the most progressive and aggressive states in terms of higher education policy and change" (McGuinness 1995: 4). Conditions changed, beginning in 1990, with an economic contraction and new political priorities. These led, in 1994, to Governor Whitman proposing to abolish the DHE and reduce the state's control.

The DHE was replaced by the New Jersey Commission on Higher Education (CHE), established to plan, coordinate, and advocate for higher education.[5] Included in its purview were 31 public and 32 independent colleges and universities. In 1994, it was governed by ten public members, appointed with the advice and consent of the Senate. Four were appointed by the Governor, and two each by the Senate President and Assembly Speaker. The chair of the Presidents' Council – a body made up of all the presidents of schools of higher education that receive direct state aid plus four presidents representing the other eleven degree-granting schools – served ex officio. Two students would also serve ex officio. In 1999, the CHE was reduced to eleven members, with six appointed by the Governor, plus one additional appointee who is a faculty member. A second ex officio official added was the chair of the Board of the Higher Education Student Assistance Authority. Senate and Assembly leaders had their appointees reduced to one each. The Commission's responsibilities include licensing institutions, approving new academic programs, reviewing budget requests, communicating with the federal government, approving capital projects, and making recommendations to the Governor and Legislature on collective bargaining and student assistance.[6]

The New Jersey Higher Education Act of 1994 that imposed all these changes was enacted relatively quickly, under a new Governor enjoying large majorities in both legislative houses. Public opposition came mainly from the outgoing

5 New Jersey was the first among a number of states that took steps to downsize the agencies that oversaw higher education (McGuinness 1995: 1) resulting in the 1994 New Jersey Higher Education Restructuring Act.

6 In dealing with its employees, UMDNJ was bound by New Jersey Public Employer-Employee Relations Act. UMDNJ workers were considered public rather than civil service employees, meaning that, although they were covered by the same health and pension plans as other state employees, they were not subject to the same state contracts or civil service rules.

Board of Higher Education and its chancellor, conducted through the Newark *Star Ledger*, but with little impact. However, the legislature did acknowledge some need to limit the Governor's authority over higher education policy (McGuinness 1995: 10).

Trustees

State oversight of UMDNJ was, after the 1994 restructuring, restricted to its own Board of Trustees. Trustees were unpaid and served a five year term. Although they were expected to be representative of the regional and demographic makeup of the state, they did so rather narrowly, through their connection with the locales of schools and institutes and the political interests identified with those areas. Their roles were seen as similar to those of corporate boards of directors. That is, they could approve and ratify, but not initiate, policies, while providing oversight over hiring, contracts and expenditures, and the institution of new programs. In effect, however, Boards acted to rubber stamp administrative initiatives.

After the federal monitor began his investigative oversight, the size of the Board of Trustees was increased from 11 to 19. Two were appointed after recommendation by the Senate president, as were two others recommended by the Speaker of the Assembly. The remaining 15 were appointed by the Governor with the advice and consent of the Senate. In combination with the resignations that followed Governor Codey's executive order that prohibited the boards as well as the presidents of all 31 state colleges, universities, and county colleges from engaging in any kind of business with their respective schools (Sherman and Heyboer 2005), Governor Corzine, taking office in 2006, could virtually remake the Board with 12 out of 15 appointments. Those came from the legal community, medicine, business, and academia, with little sign of overt political connections. Only Dr Harold Shapiro, former president of Princeton University, appeared to have a suspicion of conflict through his simultaneous membership on the Board of Overseers of RWJMS. Holdovers on the Board, vice-chair Eric S. Pennington, a municipal court judge and a Governor Whitman appointee, and two appointed by Governor McGreevy, were now a distinct minority. The remaining, ex officio, member was Fred M. Jacobs, who was appointed Commissioner of the Department of Health and Senior Services by Governor Codey.

Up to at least the time when the federal monitor took charge, all trustees could be considered patronage appointments and they manifested widespread conflicts of interest, documented in Chapter 2. Since then, there is no evidence that patronage totally disappeared. But reforms did mean reaching out to broader segments of the community and the downplaying of partisan interests.

Center for Medicare and Medicaid Service

The Center for Medicare and Medicaid Services (CMS) is the federal agency within the Department of Health and Human Services that administers Medicare and works with individual states on the provision and shared financing of Medicaid. In these capacities, CMS provides teaching hospitals with guidelines for billing charges for teaching physicians, interns, and residents and requirements for appropriate forms of documentation for services provided. As complaints surfaced about how university teaching hospitals were, in fact, billing for medical services, the Inspector-General for the Department of Health and Human Services began auditing those hospitals in 1995. Evidence of improper billing would then be turned over to the Justice Department for redress.

As described in Chapter 2, double billing and upcoding at University Hospital first began in 1993. However, the Justice Department did not begin its investigation of UMDNJ until 2005. The time lapse was presumably tied to CMS's heavy reliance on whistle blowing as a prelude to the investigation of complaints about non-compliance with its guidelines (Department of Justice 2009). Such complaints had been slow to come from within UMDNJ, for reasons explored in the preceding chapter. The resources that CMS could provide the University were so great and the consequences of their loss so grave, that both efforts to gain as much of those resources as possible, even if they were illegally obtained, and efforts to hide misdeeds so critical, that UMDNJ administrators were willing to take their chances that skirting or disregarding regulations would be undetected.

Oversight Effectiveness

The result of restructuring in 1994 left UMDNJ to conduct its business under loose state supervision. The Commission of Investigation appointed by Governor Codey in 2005, though stimulated by the abuses uncovered at UMDNJ, found "*an entire system* vulnerable to problematic governance, serious shortcomings in oversight, accountability and transparency and outright violations of the public trust" (State Commission of Investigation 2007: 1). This state of affairs, it concluded, was due to abolition of the Department of Higher Education and, with it, consistent and meaningful state oversight. From the perspective of the present analysis, the resources that the Commission on Higher Education could use to influence UMDNJ were real but had little apparent relation to either directly providing opportunities for corruption or inhibiting those that existed through other network relations.

In the for-profit world, UMDNJ's Board of Trustees would be considered a weak board of directors. It was unwilling or unable to play a strong supervisory role, remaining beholden to those responsible for its appointment and acquiescent to everything proposed by the University administration. That is, when decisions were required to allow actions to go forward, real power resided in the University (as it did in the elected government). To the extent trustees commanded resources, they were used primarily to obtain tangible rewards for themselves, their relatives, businesses with which they had ties, and local communities.

The most powerful oversight rested with the federal government through its capacity to fund graduate medical education and patient care. But because adherence to federal guidelines has been dependent on the self-reports by the supervised educational institutions, who are required to keep track of and pass on large amounts of data, there can be numerous opportunities for false reporting. Reports were a way to manipulate signals, as Vaughan (1982: 375) has described. Even without deliberate attempts to subvert federal regulations, UMDNJ could have sought to test the limits of those regulations and their enforcement through a process of gaming by searching for loopholes and ambiguities as well as perceived weaknesses in enforcement.[7] Faced with the rich resources of the federal government, UMDNJ countered with its resource of information. By manipulating that information for its own benefit, the University was able, for a considerable time, to evade the oversight capabilities of CMS.

Professions as Accrediting Bodies

Professional Control

Medicine is the archetype of a professional occupation – based on expert and specialized knowledge, the practice of which is bound by technical and ethical standards, and directed to managing its own body of knowledge and work (Freidson 1988). When states have sought to regulate professions, the latter have successfully fought back. As a result, professions have acquired state-protected rights to enforce their own authority and have used the state to help in enforcement. This medical model of a profession prevails among other university-trained health-care occupations. The assumptions flowing from participation in such professions are that members will be committed to using their expertise honestly and impartially, in the service of their patients.

7 Slater (2010) describes such gaming in the private sector and notes its connection with corruption.

In other words, professional norms should constrain unethical behavior. But counter-intuitively, Kouchaki (2013), in a series of experiments, shows that self-conceptions of professional status may make one more unethical. Her argument is that attachment to a profession means valuing its status and power, not necessarily its ethical premises.

For professionals employed in organizations, there can be an inherent tension between commitments to autonomy and organizational job requirements. But, ideally, it is a professional code of conduct that is expected to prevail, a position supported by UMDNJ's Office of Ethics, Compliance and Corporate Integrity, a unit set up in response to the abuses uncovered by the federal monitor. Students in health care fields are socialized into appropriate professional conduct, including its ethical components, through formal class instruction, most often now in courses relating to research, and in their introduction to patient care. Licensing exams for graduates typically ask for knowledge of and commitment to each profession's ethical code. Taking the Hippocratic Oath was the public symbol of that commitment, though today most medical schools do not require their students to do this.

At the same time as students are presumed to be learning ethical ways of responding to medical issues, they are exposed to an informal and hidden curriculum tied to the practices that they observe and the cultural cues they receive on how to respond to conflicting demands, some of which will undermine ethical commitments (Hafferty and Franks 1994). In addition, and in line with Kouchaki's argument, the high cost of medical education and the large debts incurred by its students point graduates away from ethical concerns that emphasize probity and patient care to those that value business success. In combination, these trends constrain efforts to inculcate ethically-responsible behavior in future practitioners (Hafferty 1998).

Professional associations play a critical role in legitimizing university programs at least equal to the regulatory authority of the states in which they are located. They do so because they have been granted official state recognition to compel universities to meet their standards. Standards apply to universities as a whole as well as to component schools and programs. In its entirety, UMDNJ came under the jurisdiction of the Middle States Commission on Higher Education (MSCHE). Its three medical schools required accreditation by either the Liaison Commission on Medical Education, administered jointly by the Association of American Medical Colleges and the American Medical Association, or the Commission on Osteopathic College Accreditation, administered by the American Osteopathic Association. Other schools, like Dentistry and Nursing, as well as specific speciality programs, came under the purview of

25 additional accrediting agencies, of which 15 were approved by the U.S. Secretary of Education.

MSCHE is a non-governmental association that confirms the authority of its member colleges and universities through evaluations of how well they conform to preconditions for appropriate administration, faculty and student qualifications, and physical and financial resources. Prior to on-site visits by evaluators appointed by the Commission, each university prepares a self-study that is the basis for MSCHE reviews of accreditation status. These are done at least every five years. In addition, MSCHE makes recommendations when changes occur, such as the introduction of a new degree program or the acquisition of a new site. UMDNJ was first accredited by MSCHE in 1979.

Beginning with the time frame central to this analysis, the first relevant period for MSCHE review was 1999–2000. That time covered the Periodic Review Report submitted by the University and its acceptance and reaffirmation of accreditation by the Commission. The next evaluation visit was scheduled for 2004–2005. By then, information about problems had come to the surface and a site visit in April, 2005 led to a decision to postpone continued accreditation until the university could document:

> (1) efforts to address financial concerns including, but not limited to, internal financial control mechanisms, and submission of results from independent financial and management audits conducted in the 2005–06 year; and (2) full implementation by the Board of Trustees of all appropriate conflict-of-interest policies and institutional compliance with MSCHE integrity standards.
>
> MIDDLE STATES COMMISSION 2010

The University's report was to have been submitted by March 1, 2006 but UMDNJ was then under the supervision of a federal monitor. In June 2006, the Commission placed it on probation. A monitoring report was then requested, due by October 15, 2006, documenting what the university was doing to address: "(1) financial concerns previously identified, (2) stabilization and reformation of the institution's Board and executive leadership, and (3) appropriate oversight and control over the institution and its activities" (Middle States Commission 2010).

The Commission continued its contacts with UMDNJ through reports and visits until removing the university from probation on March 13, 2008. That decision was made in recognition of efforts toward bringing about change. Yet more remained to be done. The University was requested to provide, by October 1, 2009, further documentation that progress was being made in redressing problems with finances, board and executive leadership, oversight and control, and in the creation of a culture of integrity. That would be followed by the usual Periodic Review Report on June 1, 2012. The 2012 reaffirmation of accreditation was qualified by notice that the Commission needed to approve any substantive changes that might be implemented in the new settings to which UMDNJ's schools and programs would be relegated after its formal dissolution.

Among accrediting bodies dealing with specialized aspects of medical education is the American Council for Graduate Medical Education (ACGME). It is a non-profit council that evaluates and accredits medical residency programs in the United States. Member organizations are the American Board of Medical Specialities, American Hospital Association, American Medical Association, Association of American Medical Colleges, and the Council of Medical Specialty Societies, each of which appoint four representatives to serve on a board of directors. Twenty-six specialty areas come under the purview of its review committees, with separate committees for a special one-year transitional-year clinical program and for institutional review. The latter two committees are appointed by the executive committee and confirmed by the board of directors; the speciality committees are appointed by the AMA Council on Medical Education and the relevant speciality boards. ACGME insures compliance by spelling out standards and requiring medical schools to prepare regular internal reviews, later matched by its own site visits (ACGME 2007). Residency programs that do not measure up can receive warnings or be placed on probation. In is dealings with UMDNJ, ACGME treated each of the two allopathic medical schools (NJMS and RWJMS) separately.

The Commission on Health Science (2004: 25), chaired by Dr Vagelos, reported that, as of July 2002, NJMS had received warnings about five of its residency programs and two were on probation. RWJMS received warning letters for two programs at its New Brunswick campus and one at its Camden campus but no programs were placed on probation. Commissioners also reported on comparisons with five top state schools, of which none had programs on probation. Although numbers of cases were small, it still appeared that UMDNJ had a poorer record than its peers. That evaluation was confirmed by later ACGME reports in which, between 2003 and 2005, five programs at NJMS were censured along with one at the Camden campus of RWJMS. Programs affected were allergy and immunology, anaesthesiology, dermatopathology, plastic surgery, and thorasic surgery at NJMS and diagnostic radiology at Camden (Stewart 2005a). Among deficiencies noted when NJMS lost its accreditation to provide cardiothoracic training were a case load too low to give sufficient experience and the failure of two of three of its graduates to pass the written examination that confers board certification (Stewart 2005c).

Professional Rewards

Professional associations command multiple resources that affect practitioners and the organizations in which they work in the most fundamental ways. Through their success in assuming governmentally-validated authority, they captured the power to determine who has the right to offer professional services, train future practitioners, and assume the identity of a specialized school of higher education. Only that validation allows individuals and schools access to financial resources necessary to carry out their responsibilities. Additionally, validation brings rewards of status, lending individuals and schools the esteem accorded the professions. Esteem, in turn, colors evaluations of faculty and their schools as they compete for recognition.

Given the overriding importance of what professional associations can offer, those receiving their benefits are expected to reciprocate with sustained adherence to their standards. But, to a considerable extent, once practitioners and schools have received initial acceptance into the professional fold, they can tap a reservoir of continuing support that tends to allay suspicion of misconduct. And it was largely the case that most UMDNJ faculty did adhere to the professional standards they had promised to uphold. When difficulties arose, it was because MSCHE relied on self-reports that were dependent on university administrators' integrity in providing trustworthy data. But the latter, while protecting the university and its programs, could engage in signaling behavior that distorted information. Only investigations by the Justice Department and the federal monitor provided the facts that would undermine the university's purported claims about how it operated. The ACGME's fact-finding abilities differed because it was able to directly assess results of board certification examinations that were given outside the University's supervision. Those results augmented UMDNJ's internal differences by revealing the greater vulnerability of NJMS compared to RWJMS.

Status-Conferring Agents

Universities are noteworthy for the extent to which they are identified by their status. It is for this reason that I have placed resources of status on an equal footing with those of power and money. Strong incentives to increase those latter resources extend to similar incentives to improve universities' repute.

How status is measured depends on the perceptions of those making the evaluations. For some, it will be determined by the success of a university's sports teams. Others may look to the size of its endowment. More conventional academic frameworks look at status in terms of faculty accomplishments. The general public is accustomed to view university status through the lens of rating agencies that take into account both faculty and students as well as such assets as the size of libraries. Most useful for this research are ratings of faculty accomplishments and peer rankings. I also take advantage of the way data were reported to discern differences in status among schools within UMDNJ.

Research Rewards

When faculty status is considered a critical component in the comparative evaluation of research universities, one measure is the amount of funding that faculty members are able to procure for their research projects. For this purpose I focus on grants from the National Institutes of Health (NIH), the principal and most prestigious agency for awards in medicine and related fields. This information also allows comparison within UMDNJ, particularly between its two principal medical schools. The results reflect how schools' externally-validated status had implications for relations within UMDNJ's core organization, in particular, by reinforcing its fragmentation.

To give greater context for the period around which abuses were found, Table 5.1 presents NIH awards in each of four fiscal years. Overall, as the university moved from one century to the next, it showed sizable gains in research funding, distributed across six of its schools. The two allopathic medical schools together were the research leaders, accounting for at least 90 percent of the dollars awarded in each of the years examined. To the extent that NIH awards translated into status, UMDNJ gained this largely through those medical schools. At the same time, those awards served as an indicator of continuing internal status differences. RWJMS, though slightly smaller than NJMS, remained the leader both in the numbers of grants awarded and in their dollar amounts. But differences within schools were not always reinforcing, as comparisons of two departments indicate. In 2005, NIH awarded NJMS almost 6.9 million dollars in five grants for its surgery department, ranking it eighteenth in the country for dollars gained. RWJMS ranked twenty-sixth, winning funding for eleven grants and a total of almost 3.7 million dollars. Of NIH grants to pediatric departments in that year, RWJMS was successful in gaining funding for twelve grants with a total just over 4.6 million compared to NJMS's over 2.5 million in five grants (Residentphysician 2009).

TABLE 5.1 *NIH awards for selected years*

School	Year	Number	$ Amount
RWJMS	1994	104	19,447,919
	1998	140	31,211,879
	2002	169	46,638,316
	2006	152	55,999,871
NJMS	1994	90	17,754,619
	1998	66	18,219,560
	2002	113	37,163,645
	2006	113	43,306,665
SOM	1994	7	910,781
	1998	8	1,931,329
	2002	10	2,845,967
	2006	4	1,368,724
Public Health	1994	0	0
	1998	0	0
	2002	10	4,487,572
	2006	10	4,113,078
Dentistry	1994	0	0
	1998	0	0
	2002	4	1,059,267
	2006	11	2,786,199
Nursing	1994	0	0
	1998	0	0
	2002	1	330,692
	2006	1	397,745

SOURCE: REPORT.NIH.GOV.INDEX.CFM

Other attempts to compare the status of the two medical schools were made by the State Commission (2007: 19).[8] NIH funding for NJMS and RWJMS in fiscal year 2001 was compared in three ways: with the top state school

8 The commissioners also measured status by counting research publications, which they appear to have averaged for both schools separately rather than summed. If they had done the latter, UMDNJ would have looked similar to Ohio State University Medical Center but still well below two other major, free-standing state medical centers, the University of

average, all state schools' average, and all allopathic schools' average, of which the last is most relevant to us. UMDNJ's two medical schools combined received 84.8 million dollars, putting the university ahead of the 70.2 million average for all allopathic schools. When comparisons are made using the latter's median of 46.5 million, UMDNJ appeared even stronger. (The difference between the mean and median indicate the large variation among state-supported medical centers). Based on absolute numbers, NJMS ranked 67th and RWJMS ranked 61st. If they had been treated as one, UMDNJ would have received a considerably higher ranking.

Status based on research awards is tied to many factors, including the cumulative ability of universities to build on past successes, their relative size and wealth, prior investments in research facilities, and the presence of new research initiatives by the state, university, or private funders. Given that none of these has been factored into this status assessment of UMDNJ, we have no clear standards by which to judge it. But based on the information at hand, it is fair to conclude that UMDNJ was a middle-ranking institution showing signs of moving up in status.[9] It was gaining recognition through efforts expended by research faculty, administrative support, and attested to by peer reviews that were difficult to manipulate. Of the two traditional medical schools, RWJMS may have had a slight edge in prestige based on research funding. In addition, in noting that faculty members did poorly in comparison to the top tier of state universities with regard to membership in honorary societies, the State Commission (2007: 18) found that RWJMS had one more such membership than NJMS.

Rankings

Prestige is common currency in the world of higher education – a way for universities to differentiate themselves; to attract students, faculty, and donors; and to give graduates a claim to recognition even without any other sign of achievement. It is hardly surprising, then, that published rankings have become a widely used means of locating the relative position of schools. The best known of these appears annually in *U.S. News and World Report* (*USNWR*), whose popularity has been matched by sharp criticisms of its methodology (e.g., Ehrenberg 2003). Two particularly troublesome aspects of its rankings are

Texas Southwestern Medical Center (UTSMC) and the University of California at San Francisco (UCSF) (State Commission 2007: 20). UTSMC was much smaller and UCSF much larger than UMDNJ.

9 The State Commission's (2007: 26–36) assessment included all of UMDNJ's schools and they appeared similar in status to the two medical schools but without the same credibility in establishing the University's overall status.

reliance on self-reported data[10] and on perceived prestige as reported by peers.[11] Assessments of prestige by peer universities are made in a context of invidious comparisons, inviting ways to game the system. The most common way to do this is by reversing the expected rankings of schools, giving the stronger ones lower ratings and the weaker ones higher ratings.

Out of 125 medical schools graded, *USNWR* did not find either NJMS or RWJMS in the top fifty between 2000 and 2005,[12] although RWJMS did receive recognition among the top fifty primary care medical schools, ranking 42 in 2000 and 47 in 2003. Neither of UMDNJ's two primary teaching hospitals, University Hospital in Newark attached to NJMS, and Robert Wood Johnson University Hospital (RWJUH) in New Brunswick attached to RWJMS, made it into the top 40 hospitals in 1995. However, by 2009, RWJUH ranked 36 in heart and heart surgery, 40 in cancer, and 50 in respiratory disorders while University Hospital ranked 44 in ear, nose and throat (*U.S. News & World Report* 2009).

Taken at face value, these rankings left both medical schools with only modest signs that they had won recognition for their quality. Although *USNWR* ranking methods are often disparaged and there is evidence that some schools have successfully manipulated their position, it does not appear that UMDNJ did anything that would have helped change its ranking.

Gaining Status

Whether measured by research grants or external rankings, both appeared to be fairly robust indicators of status. Relatively safe from blatant attempts at manipulation, they left UMDNJ with no more than a middle level of prestige when compared to other medical schools. They also confirmed the dominance of the two allopathic medical schools in establishing the University's overall status, including their claim to additional resources within UMDNJ. And of those two schools, there were signs that RWJMS received slightly higher standing than NJMS. But overall, UMDNJ's relative prestige was a limiting factor in its ability to influence its network partners.

We can better understand the significance of status when it is placed in the context of how organizations deal with dependency. One way is to buffer their core – the essential character of how an organization is defined – from outside

10 Houry's (2013) criticisms of college rankings note that some colleges have admitted to inflating scores of incoming students.

11 In the case of medical schools, peer assessments and residency director assessments each make up 20 percent of the weight assigned to overall rankings.

12 For access to these data, I am indebted to Ryan Raffery, regional assistant librarian, Library of the Health Sciences, University of Illinois, Champaign-Urbana.

interference (Scott and Davis 2007: 128–129). But how can state universities, dependent on their legislatures for existence and on their communities for the acceptance of their educational and service goals, buffer themselves from interference from these actors? The most effective strategies, used by such distinguished exemplars like the Universities of Michigan or California, are through fostering their own unique resource of reputation. They cannot do this alone, to be sure, but must rely on the financial and political resources of the state and the community to build that reputation. But once they have translated those resources into attracting a distinguished faculty along with well-qualified students, they are in a position to gain even more status. When a university can subsequently win recognition for its standing among its peers, it is more likely to have a defensible core. University administrators can use public acknowledgment of their schools' status to argue for an arm's length relation with state actors. At no time, however, had UMDNJ's stature been sufficiently high to allow for such buffering strategies.

In reality, UMDNJ was not much different than other state universities. As agencies of their states, there is no way that they can be entirely independent of political and even partisan pressures. For example, the distinction accorded the University of California system was no protection during the McCarthy era, when the legislature required faculty, along with other state employees, to sign a loyalty oath (Blauner 2009). Nor has that system been immune to periodic and even severe cuts in budgets. As a result, buffering strategies are generally difficult for universities to employ. When UMDNJ attempted to use buffering illegitimately, as it did by using illegal billing procedures to build the size and stability of its financial resources, it gambled that it would not be found out, a tactic that worked only temporarily.

Community-Based Actors

Under the rubric of the community I include civic groups, local politicians, service providers, other schools and universities, and hospitals both affiliated and unaffiliated with UMDNJ. Each of these groups had a full array of resources they could use to reward or apply pressure to UMDNJ. The University, in turn, sought to gain those resources for its benefit by coopting their agents into becoming its supporters. But given the diversity among these groups, the overlap between civic organizations and local politicians and between colleges and hospitals, and the difficulty of ensuring that all relevant groups could be identified, what follows is a sampling with an emphasis on those whose interactions with the University could be, or were, a source of corruption.

Civic Groups and Local Politicians

Some groups began with the intention of helping the University and its administration. Foremost among these was the Foundation of UMDNJ, a 501(c) (5) organization established in 1973 by four Trustees to support research excellence and healthcare. The Foundation depends on private sector support and is governed by a volunteer board. The board's ties with the University were close, given that it was made up of a mix of administrators, University trustees, and representatives of alumni associations, as well as representatives of business and the professions in the state. Its most prominent activity was funding faculty research through competitive proposals. Funds were intended as seed money for initial research that would lead to proposals to NIH or as bridge money, to allow researchers to carry over projects between funding cycles. But, as an independent entity, the Foundation did not have to account for its policies. It could then give the University President money that he could use as he saw fit. As reported in Chapter 2, the Foundation was the source of President Bergen's discretionary fund, enabling him to hire a Newark power broker, Steven Adubato, to work on the University's behalf in influencing various government departments. It also gave similar funds to President Petillo, allowing continued support for Adubato's medical service agency.

Another group with interest in funding UMDNJ was the Foundation Venture Capital Group, LLC. It is a private equity group whose board includes members of major pharmaceutical and medical device companies in New Jersey along with some University administrators. Its policy is to provide early funding for new life science companies founded by or affiliated with faculty from UMDNJ. It represented one critical means for pharmaceutical and medical device companies to establish close ties with the University. Money was the resource that gave it entry, money welcomed by the University as a means to capitalize on the skills of its faculty and build connections with businesses in the state.

New construction for the College of Medicine and Dentistry of New Jersey's (CMDNJ, later UMDNJ) facilities in Newark, begun in 1971, accentuated a racial divide between a white administration and faculty and surrounding residents who were mainly African-American and Hispanic. The resulting tensions contributed to the 1967 Newark riots and to public confrontations in 1970, when residents expressed their frustrations over the College's health care and employment practices. To relieve these pressures a Board of Concerned Citizens (BCC) was founded in 1970. With a charter supported by the Board of Trustees, the BCC expanded its reach to require input from community advisory groups for all the current and projected campuses (Leevy et al. 1975). Members of the Board included local residents, faculty and administrators, and a student representative. Although created and funded by the University, the Board still saw itself as a watchdog over the Newark neighborhood surrounding the University's operations. Speaking twenty-five years after its founding, its long-time chairwoman, Mary Mathis-Ford said "We're not swayed by anybody. We work hard independently, and we raise all kinds of hell up here" (Stewart 1995). The value the University placed on the chairwoman's leadership and support was demonstrated by its willingness to pay a total of $69,000 to chauffeur her to meetings to and from her home in the Poconos after she moved from New Jersey (Sherman and Margolin 2006a).

Civic organizations connected to local politicians were seen as particularly fruitful arenas through which the University could foster supportive links. If the University provided money and status, civic groups could reciprocate with political resources, adding to the University's legitimacy as a member of the larger community in ways similar to what University-created civic organizations did. However, when organizations existed independently of the University, they were not easy to control, as the following case, previously discussed in Chapter 2, demonstrates. Women with Hats for the Cure, founded by City Councilwoman Gayle Chaneyfield-Jenkins, benefitted from $10,000 in University support. But once public records became subject to subpoena by the F.B.I., President Petillo acknowledged that the donation had been made from an account that contained state tax dollars, and therefore was a misuse of moneys restricted to state-mandated activities. In addition, it was found that the organization was not registered as a charity with the authority to solicit donations. What was initially an effort by the University to build positive ties with the community then backfired. Accompanied by supporters, Chaneyfield-Jenkins attended a Board of Trustees meeting to protest Chairwoman Delgado's halt on all charitable contributions. She defended her organization by saying its lack of official status was simply an oversight, an argument supported by Board member Donald Bradley, who was also president of the Newark City Council. Her supporters raised the conflict level further by their use of racist rhetoric in attacking Delgado and Assemblywoman Loretta Weinberg, chairwoman of the Assembly Health Committee (Margolin 2005a).

Building connections between the University and local politicians occurred in different ways, of which all that revealed signs of corruption were recounted in Chapter 2. They included making campaign donations to individuals and political organizations of both parties, using recommendations by specific politicians to assign rankings to job applicants, hiring elected officials and local power-brokers for jobs within the University, and hiring politically-connected lobbyists. In all these ways the University used its resources of money, power, and status to solidify ties with the political community. The expectation was that politicians would reciprocate with resources they controlled, an expectation fulfilled whenever legislators channeled more money to the University and local power-brokers used their power or status to ensure that the University could operate in a conflict-free environment.

Service Providers

The range of goods and services typically required over each year's operation by the University, including its hospitals and research centers, covered office supplies, food, waste disposal, scientific equipment, building construction and repairs, and telecommunication, with costs totaling multimillions of dollars. As described in Chapter 4, the University and its components were constrained in how they contracted for such goods and services by the requirement of three price quotations for relatively small purchases and formal bids for larger ones. But these requirements could be breached, evident from the examples provided in Chapter 2 of how administrators were able avoid restrictions on their ability to conduct University business.

From the perspective of service providers, the University was potentially a rich market, one that needed to be cultivated to ensure stable ties. Chapter 2 gave examples of how gifts to UMDNJ employees were used to solidify relations. Information from other universities and their teaching hospitals have revealed how large pharmaceutical and medical device manufacturers have engaged in systematic efforts to promote ongoing relations that represent millions of dollars in profits to their companies (see Chapter 3) and UMDNJ might appear to have been an especially attractive market to those companies because of a shared location in New Jersey. Their importance to the state economy was acknowledged by the presence of representatives on University and hospital boards and in the Foundation Venture Capital Group. The following chapter notes, as well, the leadership taken by pharmaceutical company executives on state-appointed committees planning the future of UMDNJ. Those plans urged closer ties between a reconstituted UMDNJ and the pharmaceutical industry as a source of economic benefit to the state (Commission on Health Science 2004). Yet, whatever other relations may have existed, they were not sufficiently troublesome to come to public attention or to the scrutiny of the federal monitor.

Schools and Hospitals

UMDNJ existed within a competitive market with other schools, universities, and hospitals, of which I deal only with the one circumscribed by the boundaries of New Jersey.[13] Successful competition, leading to increased resources, required

13 Its competitive market, in fact, extended to New York City and Philadelphia.

the University to be alert to opportunities for expansion and to take action to forestall inroads from competitors. Nursing provided one such example.

The Coalition of Concerned Nurses and the New Jersey State Nurses Association filed suit against the University for developing a joint program with Middlesex County College in New Brunswick, even though that program had been approved by the Board of Nursing (Murray 1990). However, UMDNJ was able to successfully overcome opposition. A nursing program was already present in the School of Health Related Professions when UMDNJ moved to set up a separate school in 1990, subject to the approval of the NJ Board of Higher Education and the State Board of Nursing. The school was to include an acute care nursing assistant program, an associate of science in nursing degree as a joint program with Middlesex County College, a bachelor of science in nursing degree as a joint venture with Ramapo College, and a master of science in nursing degree. Some of the units were already in operation; others would be new. There were objections from the Board of Nursing, which saw overlap with existing programs at Rutgers University and Seton Hall and feared that nursing education would now be dominated by UMDNJ (Whitlow 1990b). But the University was able to make its case and the new School of Nursing came into formal being in 1992.

Expansion also occurred through the incorporation of existing centers. For example, the Public Health Research Institute (PHRI), founded in 1941 to fight smallpox and other infectious diseases, was brought to the Newark campus from New York in 2002 to bolster the university's stature in bio-defense and infectious disease research. Located in a new Center for Public Health, where it shared facilities with the department of microbiology and molecular genetics, PHRI was treated as a tenant although seventeen of its researchers held courtesy faculty appointments, a few were teaching, and others supervised graduate students in their labs. The arrangements turned out to be sources of contention and PHRI took UMDNJ to court for not fulfilling its agreement. This was followed by the university seeking to evict PHRI for non-payment of rent. According to Lewis Weinstein, president of the institute, "UMDNJ is trying to squeeze us out. They want to take our building, take our grants, take our scientists and put us out of business as an entity. That isn't what this was supposed to be about" (Coughlin 2004). Under an initial agreement, the court halted eviction proceedings, consolidating all the issues in contention in the state's Superior Court (Campbell 2005).

One reason to build relations with other institutions was to ensure that UMDNJ had a steady stream of students. An example was a joint program with Drew University, a small liberal arts university whose president was former Governor Thomas Kean. The agreement allowed students accepted by Drew to spend three years on its own campus and then transfer to UMDNJ. There they would be able to complete a bachelor's degree in their fourth year of study and then be guaranteed admission to the medical school (*Star-Ledger* 1992a). Other colleges with which UMDNJ had agreements for early enrollment included Ramapo College, where seniors skipped their senior year and entered the schools of dentistry, health related professions, or osteopathic medicine (*Star-Ledger* 1990c). Similar arrangements existed for students from Stockton State College, although initially not extending to the School of Health Related Professions (*Star-Ledger* 1990d). By the following year, agreement had been reached for Stockton students to also have these benefits in admission to both NJMS and RWJMS (Jenkins 1991).

When acting independently was not the most feasible avenue for achieving goals in the shortest time possible, as happened when the University wanted to enhance its research capabilities and visibility, it expanded its relations with other schools in the state. In a collaborative Graduate Center, begun in 1999, the Newark campuses of UMDNJ, the New Jersey Institute of Technology, and Rutgers University allowed graduate students to share courses and research facilities, and faculty to collaborate across universities. This was similar to the partnership the three universities already had with Essex County College in developing Science Park in Newark, designed to attract technology companies that would translate university-based research into commercial ventures (Heyboer 1999).

But competition could not always be resolved in such conciliatory ways, given the higher stakes and more limited resources that affected UMDNJ's teaching hospitals. In Chapter 4, I pointed to President Bergen's unsuccessful opposition to Governor Whitman's decision, allowing Saint Barnabas Hospital to operate the Children's Hospital of New Jersey in Newark, a setting that the University claimed for itself (Scott 1998a).

Newark was the site of competition among three hospitals over performing cardiac surgery. Beth Israel Medical Center, part of the Barnabas system and a pioneer in the field; St. Michael's hospital, part of the Cathedral Healthcare System and sponsored by the Archdiocese of Newark; and University Hospital, the teaching arm of NJMS, were all described as cash-strapped although working in an extremely lucrative field. Of the three, University Hospital performed the fewest cardiac procedures, which were, over a four year period, well below the number required for state licensing. Complaints to the state by its competitors were echoed as well by Newark Mayor Sharpe James, a crucial political actor (Leusner 2000).

Rivalry among hospitals was also the case in New Brunswick, pitting Robert Wood Johnson Universisty Hospital against St. Peter's Hospital over the possible intrusion by RWJUH into St. Peter's monopoly on neonatal intensive care. That rivalry became public through a letter written by Dr Robert Knupple to Dr Harvey Holzberg, who was CEO of RWJUH and a University trustee. Knupple was both chairman of obstetrics and gynecology at RWJMS and chief of those services at St. Peter's, only blocks away from RWJUH. Like others, whose complaints were documented in Chapter 2, Knupple chafed at Holzberg's power and his moves to direct money to the benefit of RWJUH. The stimulus for conflict was a new regulation issued by the Department of Health and Human Services, now headed by a former colleague of Holzberg, that would allow any institution designated as a children's hospital, and one that applied to RWJUH, to open a neonatal intensive care unit (Stewart and Lane 2002). Ill-feeling at St. Peter's Hospital grew and culminated in a decision to terminate its affiliation with Robert Wood Johnson Medical School. Instead, it established a teaching relationship with Drexel University College of Medicine in Philadelphia (Stewart 2005b).[14]

Further example of the unstable ties between the University and related hospitals involved Cooper University Hospital, the primary teaching hospital for RWJMS's Camden campus for approximately 30 years. But when new opportunities arose through the expansion of Rowan University, Cooper joined with it to create Cooper Medical School of Rowan University, beginning its first classes in August 2012.

Relations with the Community

Relations with community actors displayed critical differences when compared with all the other sets of actors with whom UMDNJ interacted. Although most of the latter had formidable resources, with the capacity to affect the continuity of the University's operations, relations were also relatively predictable, in the sense that the requirements shaping how resources could legitimately be obtained and used were evident to participants. University personnel knew, for example, what they must do if they wanted budget approval from the state government, accreditation for new or existing programs, or funding for a research project. Such knowledge may not have guaranteed success in achieving goals but the means to reach them were reasonably well-defined. In the case of relations with community-based actors, however, there were no

14 This series of events may raise a question of whether all affiliated hospitals should be treated as part of the core rather than the network organization. Generally, it makes most sense to consider within the core only those hospitals that were designated as the primary teaching hospitals of one of the three medical schools although the following example appears to undermine this position.

such clear pathways. Moreover, in many cases, community groups wanted resources from the University much more than they were prepared to reciprocate with their own. Existing schools and hospitals were competitors for the same resources unless they could be directly incorporated into UMDNJ or otherwise more closely tied to it. Instability was then the dominant characteristic of relations between the University and its community.

Vulnerability in the Network

UMDNJ was enmeshed in a complex network made up of multiple individuals, groups, organizations, and institutions, or, in the language of network analysis, multiple actors. Although relations with each category of actor were reciprocal, the strength of the relations was determined by the magnitude and importance of the resources involved in the exchange. In the case of the first three categories of actors – state government, state oversight agencies, and accrediting bodies – the resources they commanded all had the capacity to determine the life or death of the University. The remaining two categories – status-conferring agencies and community-based actors – were less important only because they did not have the ability to produce the same critical outcomes. Taken together, UMDNJ's embedded network relations left it in a highly dependent state.

The consequences of embeddedness and dependency are assessed with respect to how the conditions faced and the responses evoked led to corruption. Embeddedness and dependency are closely intertwined empirically, with embeddedness both a major source of dependency and the avenue for dealing with it. By disaggregating the two in the following sections, I emphasize the different circumstances that lead one or the other to play a more prominent role.

Embeddedness

Chapter 3 presented the case that, in general, changes resulting in competing norms or structures allow opportunities for corruption. Viewing change through the lens of embeddedness now uncovers a more complex relationship. When UMDNJ's embeddedness in the state's regulatory authority was changed to remove a level of oversight, that allowed misconduct to emerge. This causal connection was drawn by state investigators, who saw an opening appearing after the NJ Department of Higher Education was abolished and the University's Board of Trustees was left to provide sole state oversight (State Commission of Investigation 2007). In an expansion of H_1 under conditions of embeddedness, change remains an important precursor to corruption not only from the conflicting norms and structures it generates but also when barriers to independent and unrestricted actions are lowered. When change diminished embeddedness, it also diminished its positive constraining effects.

Two contrary tendencies are inherent in institutional embeddedness, resulting either in building relations of fairness and trust or ones that encourage rent-seeking and exploitation, with the latter leading to openings for corruption. I predicted in H_3 that corrupting opportunities would be likely to appear when relations are controlled by agents with discretion to allow unfair benefits. State embeddedness, linking the University with both the legislature and its Board of Trustees, and market embeddedness, linking the University with service providers, created arenas where such discretionary powers were used.

Misconduct is stimulated by the need to secure a reliable flow of resources (supporting H_2), enabled, in turn, by building bridges to the environment either through cooptation, alliances, or mergers[15] (Scott and Davis 2007: 235–238). Cooptation was UMDNJ's preferred approach to relations with local politicians and was also the strategy most likely to open opportunities for corruption. The exchange of favors that followed would enmesh both the University and the politicians it embraced in illegal and unethical behaviors. Cooptation had this effect by lowering politicians' commitment to their state obligations and raising them to the University's inducements. Even if University administrators saw their overtures to politicians as merely protective measures that would help the University's well-being, there was virtually no way to prevent their slide into the illegal and unethical.

Cooptation was also used with independent funding groups by relying on the presence of overlapping decision-makers with a University affiliation. That overlap helped ensure that there would be mutual agreement on goals and procedures. To the extent that those ties provided opportunities for corrupt practices, they did so by allowing the University discretion in how the funds received were used.

Local civic groups that could help the University operate in a supportive environment were also subject to cooptation but with more mixed results. Eager to obtain their cooperation, the University used its resources at times in legally and ethically questionable ways. In any case, group members did not always respond with conviction that the University was serving their best interests. Whether successful or not, cooptation based on the discretionary use of resources was, as predicted in H_3, a critical pathway to corruption.

Further support for H_3 was found when the University and its service providers developed alliances that led to ongoing relations, some of which would become corrupt. These were fostered, on the part of the University, through

15 It goes without saying that these strategies can also be used in fully legitimate ways.

reliance on no-bid contracts, and, by providers, on gifts and favors to administrators. This is not to say that all such contacts had these characteristics but that the avoidance of contracts requiring bidding was an important opening for corrupt behavior.

Some form of alliance could also be found in how the University related to the legislature and to its trustees. The value of these alliances rested on their potential to build support for the University and its programs. The enhancement of the University's status that followed would, in turn, reflect favorably on those who had made it possible. But, in the case of legislative members, the formation of alliances had much in common with University efforts at coopting local politicians. In other words, the University's improper use of campaign contributions and salaried positions left the ensuing alliances equally improper.

Alliances with trustees were manifested in the latter's support for University policies. The University reciprocated by its deference to Trustee pressures for favors, another instance of how deference could open pathways to corruption, as predicted in H_9.

The prominent role played by administrators, either as an aspect of embeddedness or a reflection of the University's dependency, also enhanced their importance in creating a climate where the achievement of goals could become more important than the means used to reach them. As part of this climate, the pursuit of individual self-interest could also be encouraged. For all of this to occur, as stated in H_4, management had to set the stage for organizational misconduct.

The network embeddedness of the University and its faculty with professional associations could also be viewed as a form of alliance. But to the extent they were, professional alliances often operated implicitly, to underpin a common identity intended to further ethical behavior. This is the opposite to what was found in the previous chapter, where the lack of a collective identity within UMDNJ supported the prediction of H_6, that it would encourage competition that could become corrupt behavior. Here, instead, we find an instance where embeddedness supported adherence to ethical norms.

Because embeddedness creates multiple and complex relations, it is probably inevitable that some of them will be unreciprocated, leading to the emergence of structural holes. Structural holes give their occupants an informational advantage that can be used to block access by others. Such structural holes are present in the relations between pharmaceutical and medical device companies and those they try to influence, including university departments and administrators (e.g., Brennan et al. 2006). I was not, however, able to document either their overwhelming presence or their corrupting impact on UMDNJ. But, for many years, UMDNJ was able to take advantage of the structural holes that existed between it and the federal government, enabling it to both withhold and falsify critical data, as predicted by H_7.

Dependency

Dependence on network partners for resources, especially those needed for survival, was an overarching characteristic of UMDNJ. That dependency was especially prominent in relations with the state of New Jersey and governmental oversight agencies. As a consequence, there were powerful incentives to gain resources even when that meant breaking the law, as happened with fraudulent billing for Medicare and Medicaid, violations of the Stark Law that prohibited paying for referrals, and misrepresentation of charitable medical care to the state. Accrediting agencies also had a life-and-death impact on UMDNJ and, to the extent that relations with them were incentives for misconduct, the latter were manifested indirectly, as they were in the case of the illegal hiring of community cardiologists as a means to ward off loss of accreditation. In all these network relations, UMDNJ demonstrated the widespread applicability of H_2.

Mergers, as a form of bridging strategy, are best understood in relation to problems of dependency since they often required moving beyond existing embeddedness. UMDNJ reached out to mergers and acquisitions as a way of increasing its resources, adding other schools in the state as feeders of students and other hospitals as feeders of patients and settings for training students. Those strategies could also be ways of reducing competition for patients and for state funding, but, in themselves, they were not clear opportunities for corruption. However, since mergers and acquisitions always needed state approval, this, in turn, invited political scrutiny and the potential for collusion. Although mergers begin outside of embeddedness, in the end they may demonstrate the latter's reach, as predicted in H_3.

Lack of transparency is widely understood to be a condition allowing and even promoting corruption (e.g., Rose-Ackerman 1999), and basic to the formulation of H_5. Dependency on state and local officeholders and subsequent efforts by the University to influence them were aided to the extent that those efforts would be conducted without public scrutiny. But where transparency could not be avoided, as in the relations linking the University with the accreditation policies of the American Council of Graduate Medical Education, it prevented misconduct in reporting.

Because the volume and complexity of the data that UMDNJ's hospitals were required to transmit to the Center for Medicare and Medicaid Services (CMS) was so great, the latter had difficulty performing checks on accuracy. This left CMS to rely on the integrity of UMDNJ's reporting and opened the opportunity for UMDNJ to manipulate the signals it sent about the quality of its data. UMDNJ then banked on the expectation that its distortions would remain undetected. Further support for H_8 in how signaling could be used came from the information included in the University's self-reports to the Middle States Commission on Higher Education.

Organizational Vulnerability

Putting UMDNJ's core organization together with its network identified three characteristics that stimulated pathways to corruption. Dependency was present in both organizational milieus, a constant reminder of its vulnerability to shortfalls in resources and a continuing incentive to acquire them, no matter how many rules would be bent. In the core, the second dominant characteristic came from distortions associated with its hierarchical structure. In the network, the third was the widespread embeddedness that linked the core with its environment. Just as with dependency, both hierarchy and embeddedness opened multiple opportunities allowing corrupt practices. Taken together, all three organizational characteristics support the expectations hypothesized in Chapter 3 to account for corruption.

The strongest emphasis in this analysis has been on the importance of organizational structure in creating avenues for stimulating corruption. To the extent that culture helped explain UMDNJ's corruption, the cultural elements that were influential grew out of practices that emerged from its structure and the constraints it imposed. Although this chapter and the preceding one paid attention to the identify of those involved in corrupt behavior, explaining their roles in terms of a more general approach to individual agency was restricted to the prediction that administrators were responsible for a climate encouraging misconduct.

Linking how UMDNJ became vulnerable to corruption with similar factors affecting academic centers of health care education in the United States as well as higher education globally is the subject of the final chapter. It is halted by a digression, necessary for dealing with the circumstances that led to UMDNJ's demise. The disappearance of UMDNJ as an independent body was preceded by a number of proposals, generated under different of governors, for UMDNJ's reorganization along with the reorganization of higher education in the state. None of the proposals directly tackled problems of corruption, not surprising given that only the last one was submitted after the final report of the federal monitor. But, as I demonstrate in the following chapter, all of them are relevant to understanding corruption because of what the plans said about planners' perceptions of why change was necessary and how improvements could be realized.

CHAPTER 6

Reorganization and Breakup

Plans for Change

For most of its history, UMDNJ was the sole comprehensive academic medical center in the state. Its importance to the economic and public well-being of New Jersey had been established long before the University became enmeshed in corrupt behavior. As states came to recognize how the academic sciences could become economic engines of development (Berman 2011), New Jersey also began to pay attention. The biomedical fields were growing in prominence and New Jersey was already home to major pharmaceutical manufacturers. These conditions enhanced the potential role of medical schools in the state's economic growth. Beginning in the early 2000s, three New Jersey governors turned their attention to UMDNJ as a critical player in that growth.

The timing of each governor's proposals occurred at different phases in UMDNJ's experiences with corruption and the call for a public accounting. Governor McGreevey took office in 2002 with an existing commitment to transform the state's system of higher education but prior to any public recognition of how troubled UMDNJ already was. In 2006, Governor Corzine's interests were responsive to early reports from the federal monitor's investigation but never moved beyond an inconclusive legislative task force. As a result, they receive only cursory consideration here. Governor Christie took office in 2010 following his tenure as U.S. Attorney, when he had pledged to uncover UMDNJ's misdeeds. As governor, he was in a position to pursue his own agenda on how to remake the University. After a task force he appointed proposed the break up of UMDNJ, Christie responded with his assessment of the University:

> It was a corrupt and ineffective absolute pit of political patronage.... This move will allow the institution to fully turn the page from past missteps and the lawbreaking at UMDNJ that have cost not only the institution, but the state.
>
> CORBETT and PORTNOY 2012

Regardless of Christie's stated views, planning under his office was similar to that under McGreevey's, where the primary objective was higher education's contribution to economic development, to be achieved through enhancing the advantages of local business and political interests, and not the specific problems of UMDNJ. This does not make this chapter a digression from understanding UMDNJ's path to corruption because proposals directly addressed how higher education should best be organized. And it is organization, as the preceding chapters demonstrated, that contains the roots of whether universities will be primarily law-abiding and ethical institutions or ones succumbing to corruption. In tracing the steps leading up to UMDNJ's breakup, it becomes possible to distinguish, out of all the policies advocated, those that could reduce organizational vulnerability to misconduct. Then the policies actually implemented, juxtaposed with what existed at the host universities, and in particular Rutgers, give some insight into the road ahead for the organization that was once UMDNJ.

McGreevey's Plan

Transformation

Shortly after taking office, Governor McGreevey appointed a Commission on Health Science, Education and Training to examine health care education in the state and make recommendations for its improvement (McGreevey 2002a). Although the primary focus was on UMDNJ, the Commission (2004) also included Rutgers University and the New Jersey Institute of Technology (NJIT) in its review. Among its recommendations were the creation of a single public university system with three autonomous universities located in the northern (Newark), central (New Brunswick/Piscataway), and southern (Stratford/Camden) regions.

Acting on the Commission's recommendations, the Governor appointed a Steering Committee (McGreevey 2002b) to assess the impact of the recommendations and create a restructuring plan.[1] Like the prior Commission, the Review, Planning and Implementation Steering Committee (Steering Committee) was chaired by Dr P. Roy Vagelos, retired chairman and CEO of Merck and Company and recently appointed by Governor McGreevey to the Rutgers Board of Governors. The remaining 20 members included the Commissioner of the Department of Health and Senior Services; chairs of the Boards of Trustees of Rutgers, UMDNJ, and NJIT; the chair of Rutger's Board of Governors; presidents of Rutgers and NJIT; and the Executive Vice President

1 He also charged the Commission on Higher Education to develop a strategic plan for all of NJ's schools of higher education and appointed another Commission to develop a blueprint for economic development that would foster collaboration between universities and industries in the state.

of Academic Affairs for UMDNJ, Dr Robert Saporito. The remainder represented higher education, research foundations, business and industry, the Governor's education cabinet, and the community. Planning and coordinating of the Committee's activities were done by the Pappas Consulting Group, an organization that served other schools and universities in a similar capacity.

The objective of restructuring was oriented to the future, aimed at harnessing the potential of higher education to enhance the state's economic viability. In this goal, New Jersey was adopting a perspective, emerging in the 1980s, that university-based innovations in science and technology could further economic growth (Berman 2011: 2). The Steering Committee's identification of four critical conditions underlying its work affirmed this perspective and related it to existing measures of quality. These were:

> A low proportion of talented and diverse New Jersey students having access to the public research universities.
> A respectable level of research productivity but not at a level reached by the very best public research universities.
> A substantial risk that the state will continue to lose its competitiveness in key knowledge-based business and industry.
> A number of financial and structural issues that impede overall national competitiveness, and that limit the integration of the health sciences with other academic areas, and that decrease maximum effectiveness and efficiency.
>
> STEERING COMMITTEE 2004: 11

The Steering Committee argued that all the problems listed could be remedied by the creation of a single system, headed by a Chancellor and governed by a Board of Regents that, along with local boards, would supervise the three autonomous universities, each headed by its own President. Each of the universities would have its own medical school and equal commitment to liberal arts and sciences.

The northern university would emphasize biomedical sciences, technology, and the professions by incorporating all of NJIT, those UMDNJ schools already in Newark, and the Newark campus of Rutgers, including its business and law schools. Its mission would be focused on Newark and reflected in "targeted research, responding to the economic, cultural and social needs of the city and beyond, and delivering quality and accessible health care and education" (Steering Committee 2004: 18).

The central university, located in the New Brunswick/Piscataway region, would be a combination of Rutgers University, already the dominant presence there, along with its current neighbor, UMDNJ's Robert Wood Johnson Medical School. With this change, New Jersey would acquire "a university of international stature" (Steering Committee 2004: 29).

The southern university, anchored in Camden, would be primarily oriented to the needs of its region by increasing educational opportunities, including the addition of a number of Ph.D. programs, for an under-served population. It would draw together existing programs in arts and sciences, business, and law from Rutgers with UMDNJ's School of Osteopathic Medicine and the third and fourth years in allopathic medicine from Robert Wood Johnson Medical School, then offered in collaboration with Cooper Hospital.

Among the issues that the Steering Committee identified as key to the reorganization of the public university system were those that related to problems of governance. It concluded that what was needed was the adoption of

> a joint governance system that enables strong leadership at both the system and university level; that empowers the Chancellor and the Presidents to lead; that secures suitable insulation from inappropriate political interference; that provides exemplary accountability for both financial and academic performance; that attracts talented people to want to serve on the various boards; that increases the effectiveness of advocacy; and that enables the goals to be met and the benefits to be realized.
>
> STEERING COMMITTEE 2004: 62

With that paragraph the Steering Committee revealed its recognition of the need to counter some of the attributes I have already tied to the University's corruption: the nature of leadership, political intrusiveness, and limited accountability.

The Steering Committee placed its faith in a single comprehensive system headed by a Board of Regents that would appoint the Chancellor and validate his or her presidential appointments, budgetary requests to the State, and policies. The Chancellor's role was conceived as a powerful one: coordinating the budgetary requests and special mission of the component universities, serving as the system's spokesperson, and assuming the duty to "facilitate collaboration" and "manage competition" (Steering Committee 2004: 56). The inclusion of the latter two responsibilities presents an implicit acknowledgment of what was then missing from leadership at UMDNJ. Chapter 4 identified the low levels of colleagueship across schools and the weak sense of common purpose for UMDNJ as a whole as sources of vulnerability. The Steering Committee's proposal implied that those defects could be overcome by a different kind of leadership.

A powerful Chancellor was to be matched with powerful Presidents, each of whom was expected to assume independent responsibility for such key issues as setting tuition and fees; fund-raising; communicating with stakeholders; ensuring diversity of faculty, staff, and students; and contributing to the economic development of his or her region. Each university's Board of Trustees would, like the Board of Regents in relation to the Chancellor, validate the policies and recommendations of its President. As an important addition, each was charged with insuring "strong fiscal stewardship," another sign that the Steering Committee was mindful of the need for vigilance over financial matters.

The Steering Committee's unique and ambitious vision of what higher education in New Jersey should be concluded by affirming its commitment to a governing system with a Board of Regents, Chancellor, and Presidents but ended without recommending a final version of how governance, in practice, would work. It had conducted its investigations openly and with input from the primary players, allowing its opponents to mobilize.[2] Ultimately, that mobilization would ensure that its model for transforming public higher education would fail.

Opposition

The first obstacle to agreement on governance came from Rutgers University. Before Rutgers was created a public university in 1956, it was governed by a Board of Trustees. The 1956 law transferred governance to a Board of Governors but continued the Board of Trustees[3] in an advisory capacity along with fiduciary responsibilities over assets that existed prior to 1956 (Rutgers 2013). The Boards had the authority to approve any changes in governance affecting Rutgers and they argued for joint governance between the Chancellor/Board of Regents and the Presidents/Boards of Trustees (Steering Committee 2004: 55). Their objections were not resolved in discussions with the Governor and ultimately prevented the Steering Committee from presenting a decisive recommendation.

But, even earlier, there was vocal opposition to restructuring from local political interests. As soon as the Steering Committee was appointed, unnamed

2 The Steering Committee established subcommittees on the proposed north, central, and southern campuses to address proposed changes. Although the subcommittee reports were essentially positive in recognizing the benefits each new university would bring, they all raised major questions about funding and governance (Rutgers Focus 2003).

3 The Board of Trustees continued to be made up mainly of Rutgers alumni along with some public members elected by the Board. From among its members, it recommended nominees for the Board of Governors to the Governor.

sources found the Governor's nomination of Dr. Vagelos to Rutgers Board an "ominous" threat to UMDNJ's autonomy, while State Senator Ronald Rice, representing Essex County and the Newark site of its operations, complained that "we don't want anyone to mess with the medical school" (Campbell 2002a). Mary Mathis-Ford, chair of the UMDNJ Board of Concerned Citizens, worried that a merger with Rutgers would leave University Hospital without the means to continue caring for the poor (Campbell 2002b). Political opposition continued as public hearings began, with seven state legislators from Essex county vowing resistance (Campbell and Stewart 2002).

The hearings were also the setting for opposition from UMDNJ students and faculty members. Yet at least one person spoke up in favor of change. Arthur Ritter, associate professor of pharmacology and physiology and former head of the faculty association was reported to have said that "UMDNJ has poor leadership, does not attract strong students and has no prestige outside Newark. A Rutgers merger might do the school some good" (Heyboer and Stewart 2002).

With former Governors Thomas Kean[4] and Brendan Byrne in support of the new university system, some administrators at both UMDNJ and Rutgers were willing to take a similar stand. At UMDNJ, these were the deans of NJMS and RWJMS (Margolin and Heyboer 2002). But theirs would not become the official position. In a twelve-page response, former President Stanley Bergen Jr and then current President Stuart Cook defended UMDNJ and their opposition to restructuring by criticizing the Governor's political appointments to the Board of Trustees, the inadequacy of state funding, and the committee reports that characterized UMDNJ as merely of average quality. In defense of UMDNJ, they cited its record in training minorities and its growing success in obtaining research funding (Campbell and McCarron 2002; Peterson 2002).

Such opposition, along with the price tag that would have been entailed in creating three new university complexes, took its toll and, by the end of the following year, the Governor had put university restructuring on the back burner (Margolin and Patterson 2003).

Aftermath

Dr Vagelos, who had shaped the whole debate on restructuring and who was its strongest advocate, took the absence of a decision as a clear sign of defeat. "After two years, I have pretty well conceded that I failed.... It became clear at

---

4 Governor Kean, president of Drew University, expressed his pleasure that Governor McGreevey had named him as his top choice for the new Chancellor position (Margolin and Heyboer 2002).

the end of last year that the proposal would not move forward. We did not have leadership and board support" (Dowling 2004). He matched his disappointment by resigning from the Rutgers Board of Trustees and its Board of Governors, where he had been the only one opposed to issuing a joint statement with the Governor's office that advocated shelving the proposed changes. But he remained convinced his report would be "a road map for how to do this in the future" (Dowling 2004).

The next person to leave was Dr Stuart Cook, President of UMDNJ, who resigned in April 2004. In a generally laudatory article about Cook's qualities as a researcher and his actions as President, journalist Bob Braun noted that, while Cook had been critical of the proposed changes and warned of political interference, he had been unwilling to make his positions public. Instead, he left much of the criticism to former President Bergen. Cook "said some damning things about the future of research and the role of politics and the interests of pharmaceutical houses. But it never got out" (Braun 2004).

Later, the inconclusive effort under Governor Corzine to address the organization of higher education in the state provoked renewed attention to at least some features of the Steering Committee report. Two critically placed Democratic State Senators, Raymond J. Lesniak, representing the Union County site of UMDNJ's Scotch Plains campus, and Joseph F. Vitale, representing the Middlesex County site of the New Brunswick/Piscataway campus, both advocated UMDNJ's restructuring. They recommended either joining UMDNJ and Rutgers or creating two new universities. One of the latter would consist of all the schools currently in Newark, whether affiliated with Rutgers, UMDNJ, or NJIT. The other possible university would bring together UMDNJ's schools in Stratford (Camden County) and in New Brunswick with Rutgers's facilities in those two areas. Both were unconvinced by the federal monitor, Herbert Stern, who proposed that finding a new president for UMDNJ would be sufficient to set it on a new path. According to Senator Vitale,

> Our goal is to restore credibility to UMDNJ which, under its current administrative structure, is beyond repair...Every nationally recognized medical school and research facility is an integral part of a top-flight academic university. As a unified entity, it will compete for the best faculty, students, researchers, scientists and financial resources.
>
> New Jersey Senate Democrats News Releases 2006

But resistance remained, evident from the absence of a state resolution. Opponents of merger between UMDNJ and Rutgers could point to both parties' underlying weaknesses and inefficiencies. Unlike the case of successful private-sector mergers,

> Rutgers and UMDNJ are not lean, mean organizations. Both are heavily influenced by politics. Both are bureaucracies that lack strong managerial skills. Neither has the incentive or will to make the harsh decisions a merger would suggest.
>
> LEONTIADES 2007

Yet the two state senators, long noted for their political influence, would turn out to be among those prescient enough to recognize the appeal of major change. Although the thorough-going restructuring of public higher education envisioned by Dr Vagelos and others may have been too broad, too expensive, and too threatening of entrenched interests to become reality, the underlying model was also too potent to entirely disappear. Combining the value of medical education as a state and local asset with the convention of embedding it in a comprehensive university would continue to attract followers.

Christie's Plan

Reconstruction

In the spring following his election as Governor, Chris Christie issued an Executive Order setting up a Task Force on Higher Education. The Task Force was given a broad mandate and directed to "make recommendations to improve the overall quality and effectiveness of the State's higher education system" (Christie 2010). After setting out a list of eleven issues to be addressed, the Order specifically requested the Task Force to review requirements for University Presidents to file financial disclosure statements and for governing boards to file conflict of interest forms.[5] To carry out these activities, the Governor appointed five members to the Task Force, headed by Thomas Kean, former Republican Governor and current President of Drew University, a private university in New Jersey, who had earlier expressed his support for the restructuring plan submitted to Governor McGreevey. Others included Dr Margaret Howard, a Drew University vice president and Dr George A. Pruitt, president of Thomas Edison State College, a school that enabled adults to get degrees through on-line courses and credit for life

5 The Task Force recommended that trustees fill out one set of application forms and, once confirmed, file only conflict of interest forms (Kean 2010: 15).

experiences.[6] Completing the committee were Robert E. Campbell and John L. McGoldrick, both retired executives with pharmaceutical companies, the first with Johnson and Johnson and the second with Bristol-Myers Squibb. McGoldrick was also chairman of the Board of Trustees of the New Jersey Association of State Colleges and Universities.

The Task Force's work began after UMDNJ's misconduct had become public and the federal monitor had presented his findings. While it could draw on the previous reports issued under the direction of Dr Vagelos, there had been an important change in the educational environment. In 2009, Rowan University and Cooper University Hospital agreed to create a four-year allopathic medical school, scheduled to open in Camden in 2012. This meant that the 2004 Steering Committee's vision of a comprehensive university that included a medical school serving the southern portion of the state was beginning to take shape, but only by ignoring the presence of both UMDNJ and Rutgers. The Task Force itself appeared to be operating with a clearer sense of the political realities affecting the transformation of higher education in New Jersey. Its recommendations were consequently more restrained than those produced by the Vagelos committees. I have selected from its recommendations only those applying directly to UMDNJ and those intended to affect fiscal integrity and governance in general.

The most specific recommendation made by the Kean Task Force (2010: 66) that affected the transformation of UMDNJ was to merge Robert Wood Johnson Medical School and the School of Public Health with Rutgers University. Although acknowledging the importance of all the UMDNJ schools in Newark and the role of University Hospital in training physicians and serving the community, the Task Force left unresolved their future organization. Similarly, it made no recommendations for the treatment of UMDNJ's operations in Camden, particularly the School of Osteopathic Medicine, even while recognizing the potential of the Cooper Medical School of Rowan University to take a leading role in the area (Kean 2010: 67). At the same time, it urged support for Rutgers-Camden operations. Over all, the Task force's major emphasis was on strengthening Rutgers University, to move it from "good to great." It did not deny the urgency of UMDNJ's problems but called for them to be assigned to other committees specifically appointed to find a resolution.

The Task Force's recommendations on governance (Kean 2010: 14) were in keeping with my earlier assessments of how UMDNJ's vulnerabilities to corruption might be inhibited. Among the new features would be the elimination of

6 Although there was some discussion of including Thomas Edison in a merger with Rutgers, it remains autonomous.

the Commission on Higher Education and its replacement with a more powerful structure, headed by a Secretary of Higher Education and advised by a Governor's Higher Educational Council, staffed by the Secretary. The Secretary would have the authority to require boards of trustees to take action against conditions that could lead to college and university failure because of financial problems, fraud, or gross mismanagement.

The Task Force went on to urge that trustees be appointed on the basis of their qualifications for the job. The institutions that they oversee should be self-governing and free of partisanship. Except for Rutgers, already governed by its 1956 agreement, remaining governing boards should initiate trustee nominations and present them to the governor. All boards would be required to ensure transparency and accountability by having an audit committee, an internal auditor, and an annual audit conducted by an outside auditor.

Governor Christie's reactions to the Task Force's report affirmed his commitment to change. "You have a governor now who understands UMDNJ better than most of my predecessors.... I understand the institution and its issues and I'm already committed to transformation" (Heyboer and Gibson 2011). He followed up with the appointment of an Advisory Committee focused on UMDNJ and the future of health care education. It was chaired by Dr Sol J. Barer, the executive chairman of Celgene (Barer 2012). Other committee members were Robert Campbell, former vice chairman of Johnson and Johnson; Joyce Wilson Hartley, Essex County administrator; Anthony Perno, president and CEO of Cooper's Ferry Development Association, a non-profit agency concerned with the economic development of Camden; and Harold Shapiro, former president of Princeton University. The committee was representative of all the major stakeholders affected by the fate of UMDNJ with the exception of those directly employed or served by the University.

The Advisory Committee's principal recommendation was the creation of a single health sciences university, based in Newark, but with enhanced autonomy for some of its parts. It would include the New Jersey Medical School, the Dental School, the Graduate School of Biomedical Sciences, the School of Nursing, and the School of Health Related Professions, all in Newark. Also to be included in this university, but with some flexibility in management, were University Behavioral Health Care, the School of Osteopathic Medicine, and the Public Health Research Institute.

One of the most difficult and contentious issues that had confronted all the committees considering restructuring concerned University Hospital (UH), a longstanding financial drain on UMDNJ. The Barer committee recognized both the serious financial obligations that the hospital currently generated and the centrality of its operations for the education of health care practitioners and the needs of Newark and other Essex County residents. It recommended that UH continue as the principal teaching hospital of the restructured university under a public-private partnership, with the private partner as the manager under a long-term contractual relationship. Who that private partner might be was not identified.

> A financial firewall should be instituted between UH and the transformed health sciences university so that situations that have arisen to expediently accommodate financial shortfalls at UH and UMDNJ do not occur again. The Committee must emphasize its view that there must be instituted within the agreement noted here significant financial and management separation between the proposed New Jersey Health Science University (NJHSU) and UH, including but not limited to the recommended financial firewall. Without that separation there is little chance for change, in the Committee's view.
>
> BARER 2012: 16–7

The Barer Report agreed to the benefit of a merger between Rutgers University and RWJMS along with the inclusion of the School of Public Health and an expanded Cancer Institute of New Jersey (Barer 2012: 26–29). It viewed the existing expansion of Rowan University into Camden as a welcome development and recommended that Rutgers University's Camden operations be united under Rowan's jurisdiction (Barer 2012: 23–25). Yet it held a different perspective on where the School of Osteopathic Medicine should be administered, opting for its continued inclusion in the remade operations of UMDNJ in Newark, which they named New Jersey Health Sciences University (NJHSU), but with substantial autonomy (Barer 2012: 21–22). Overall, it concluded that Newark stood to benefit from a change in the current collaborative practices of all the public institutions of higher education in that city. To do so, the latter needed to "expand, commit to, and *formalize* an existing but faltering collaborative enterprise to enhance their programs and services as well as positively affect the city's economic, cultural and educational future" (Barer 2012: 19, emphasis in the original).

No matter what would be done about higher education in the state, UMDNJ could not continue as it was.

> ...it is the Committee's judgment that there are strong arguments for a set of new and revitalized institutions and organizational affiliations since it will be very difficult for UMDNJ as it currently exists to ever fully recover its reputation.

> The historic accumulation of inappropriate practices, the resultant negative goodwill and a cumbersome administrative structure continue to represent a burden both to the morale of UMDNJ's many talented staff and to UMDNJ's capacity to continue to enhance its programs.
>
> BARER 2012: 27

Reactions

The first official reaction to the Kean report was a negative one from UMDNJ. President William F. Owen Jr, in opposition to merger with Rutgers, cited the loss of 20 percent of the University's current funding if RWJMS were gone, with the potential for more losses (Jones 2011). In addition, the fate of University Hospital was a critical concern. According to Dr Owen, "The impact on the hospital is something that really frightens me" and State Senator Loretta Weinberg, chair of the Senate health committee, agreed that the protection of University Hospital was "a very, very big deal" (Stainton 2011). Most dismissive was the response of UMDNJ employees. A Joint Analysis (2011), issued by the American Federation of Teachers NJ State Federation, NJ State Conference of the American Association of University Professors and Hospital Professionals and Allied Employees of NJ, took issue with the very nature of the Task Force Report.

- The Task Force Report is self-serving. It is written by presidents and board members for presidents and board members.
- The Task Force Report incomprehensively argues for both, more public support for higher education and, at the same time, less public accountability....
- The Task Force Report dismisses as a myth the costs of duplicate and disparate programs and systems across institutions of higher education, while the State of New Jersey is going in exactly the opposite direction–streamlining and sharing services and systems to save costs.

Governor Christie accepted the Barer committee report and announced his intention to submit an executive reorganization plan to the legislature. Reporting on the proposed changes, Corbett and Portnoy (2012) observed, "The ambitious new plan carries with it political overtones, in both the effective dismantling of parts of UMDNJ and the shifting of resources to South Jersey." But the Governor was quick to refute that possibility.

> Christie denied George Norcross, the Camden County power broker and chairman of Cooper University Hospital who worked behind the scenes

> for years to gain approval of the new medical school at Rowan, had a major role in the proposed restructuring. "Look behind the curtains back there. He ain't back there, OK?" Christie said during Wednesday's press conference. "Mr. Norcross is a significant player in public life in South Jersey and across the state. Did I speak to him? I did not. Did he influence the process? I have no idea".
>
> CORBETT and PORTNOY 2012

For others, however, the Barer recommendations were no more welcome than previous ones. At a joint hearing before both houses of state government, Newark Mayor Cory Booker was unremitting in his criticisms. In contrast to proposals for the southern and central parts of the state, where medical education would be part of two comprehensive universities, he alleged that Newark's institutions would be left without such a foundation, relegating them to "second class" status. Along with residents of his city, he expressed concern about the future of University Hospital. Also rising to the defense of Newark, its university and hospital, was George Hampton, a former UMDNJ Vice President of Urban Planning and Development, who compared the proposed changes to a "hostile corporate takeover" (O'Dea 2012).

But the current UMDNJ administration behaved as though the battle over the University's breakup had been lost and nothing would be gained by opposition. Denise V. Rodgers, acting UMDNJ president, was described as "resigned to a restructuring" and, of the deans who testified, "when pressed by legislators, none was willing to publicly oppose the restructuring" (O'Dea 2012).

Resolution

To this point, both support and opposition were directed to recommendations that were still incomplete. Following the Governor's agenda, it would be up to the legislature to formally remake public higher education, accomplished with the New Jersey Medical and Health Sciences Education Restructuring Act (2012). The direct effect on UMDNJ was to transfer all of its units to Rutgers University with two exceptions. University Hospital would become a separate non-profit legal entity while remaining the principal teaching hospital for all Newark-based operations of the newly enlarged Rutgers. The School of Osteopathic Medicine and all operations in Stratford would be transferred to Rowan University, with the understanding that there would still be shared space arrangements with UMDNJ/Rutgers until further negotiations. The UMDNJ additions to Rutgers led to the creation of a new school, Rutgers Biomedical and Health Sciences (RBHS) that would also encompass Rutgers existing schools of Nursing and Pharmacy and the Institute of Health, Health Policy and Aging Research.

These changes required new forms of governance. Rutgers formerly had three Chancellors heading its three campuses. Now, in addition to the Chancellor who headed Rutgers's existing schools in Newark,[7] a second Chancellor would be added to head RBHS, with both chancellors based in Newark and reporting to the President. RBHS itself would have two provosts, one for schools in Newark and the other for those in New Brunswick. RBHS was to be supported through a separate line item in the annual appropriations.

The most striking feature of the 2012 Education Restructuring Act is that it became a reality. Unlike McGreevey's elaborate plan or Corzine's short-lived one, Governor Christie was able to bring his vision of public higher education to the legislative test. Credit for the achievement of his goal must be given to his own commitment to change, aided by the sorry example that UMDNJ's history provided. But his predecessors' plans also helped by opening new ways of looking at the distribution of educational opportunities in the state. Perhaps most important, though, was the partisan consensus that the new arrangements aroused. Although the Governor, a Republican, dismissed the possibility that there was any influence from politicians and their local agendas, it is not irrelevant the three primary sponsors and one co-sponsor of the Senate bill and the four sponsors and four co-sponsors of the Assembly bill were all Democrats. The changes, as they saw them, were good for their districts, encompassing the New Brunswick and Newark sites of UMDNJ and Rutgers and the Glassboro and Camden sites of Rowan University. The latter district was represented by Senate sponsor Donald Norcross, brother of power broker George Norcross.[8]

Death and Afterlife

UMDNJ's Demise

Once a legislative solution had been agreed on, opposition from UMDNJ administrators, faculty, and supporters virtually disappeared. One critical voice remained in Dr Michael P. Riccards, executive director of the NJ Hall

7 These include arts and sciences, law, business, nursing, public affairs, criminal justice, and a graduate school.

8 The latter "Norcross didn't invent machine politics, but he raised it to a fine art form" (Ingle and McClure 2008: 88).

Institute of Public Policy. Riccards (2012b) zeroed in on some unresolved weaknesses in the new arrangements.

> There is some belief that Rutgers will become stronger and so will the medical school in the north if they are administratively entangled. But medical schools are administrative nightmares, especially in this time of accelerating demands, aging populations, and controversial federal oversight. The medical school of the north is especially plagued by the immense patronage demands of the Essex county delegation.... The merger of the School of Osteopathic Medicine and Rowan College (now University) really make little sense except as way to increase the southern Jersey profile for its political leaders....as the Miami University of Florida has shown, medical schools are horrendously expensive, unmanageable almost by their nature, and inherently poorly managed. And they inhabit a different world from universities, colleges, and more mundane research.

On July 1, 2013, when the Medical and Health Sciences Restructuring Act took effect, UMDNJ ceased to exist as a separate organization. The emergence of two newly enlarged public universities was celebrated with special events and new signage. Anticipation of financial benefits added to the excitement.[9]

But even with attention shifting to the remade universities, concerns remained about the costs and governance of Rutgers. *The Record* (2013a) of Bergen County compared the results to sausage making.

> ...sausage making is never pretty, and Christie, Norcross and the political supporters of the merger...held to the belief that the public would be better off not knowing what went into the sausages. The complete costs of this merger are still not clear. Rutgers is expected to absorb $76 million of the estimated $100 million cost of the merger.

As the editors predicted, Rutgers quickly raised its tuition for the 2014–15 academic year. Because its Board of Trustees, providing a link with the University's independent past and unencumbered with political appointees, had been in the forefront of arguing successfully against those provisions of the merger that would have given its schools in Camden to Rowan University, the Board

9 The town of Glassboro welcomed the growth potential of Rowan University by rebuilding its town center, begun in 2009 in anticipation of the University's success in expanding its size and influence (Kaysen 2013).

came under political attack from State Senate President Sweeney, Democrat from Gloucester County, the seat of Rowan University. Sweeney moved to abolish the Board of Trustees and, though his initial efforts failed (Friedman and Heyboer 2013), *The Record* (2013a) predicted that there would be continued pressure to do away with the Board because "Cynics, including us, see this as an attempt to silence opposition, not an effort to streamline governing bodies."

Perpetuating Conditions

The UMDNJ that merged with Rutgers and Rowan was not, after undergoing internal reorganization under pressure from the federal monitor, accrediting agencies, and public outrage, the same institution that had existed during the height of its illegal and unethical activities. Well before its breakup, the lessons learned by UMDNJ from its scandalous past were already incorporated into remedial rules and regulations aimed at specific practices related to hospital billing, letting of contracts, and conflicts of interest. To those who moved with UMDNJ to either Rutgers or Rowan, corruption may now be only an uncomfortable memory. Yet left intact were some fundamental sources of UMDNJ's past vulnerability.

Whatever has been carried over from UMDNJ remains relevant because of the powerful effects of formative experiences. As Panebianco (1988: xiii) observes, "the way in which the cards are dealt out and the outcomes of the different rounds played out in the formative plan of the organization, continue in many ways to condition the life of the organization even decades afterwards." Stinchcombe's (1965: 160) analysis of this "imprinting" finds three possible reasons for why structures and practices continue. It could be due to the inherent efficiency of the structure; the absence of competitive pressure to change; or the impact of tradition, vested interests, or external ideologies. Although one could assume that traditions and vested interests would be the main avenues of continuity in the case of UMDNJ, existing structures, regardless of their efficiency, and the monopolistic nature of state enterprises are also likely to play a role.

By comparing proposals made by Governor-appointed planning committees, the final enabling legislation, carry-overs from UMDNJ, and conditions at Rutgers, the major new home of UMDNJ, we can begin to assess the possible impact of the merger on future vulnerability to corruption. I divide changes into how they are likely to affect the three principal sources of vulnerability.

Effects on Hierarchy

The establishment of governance arrangements in the Education Restructuring Act recognized the collective identity of all the health-related fields and assembled them into a new school, Rutgers Biomedical and Health Sciences (RBHS). Although it is doubtful that any alternative was feasible, the segregation of medicine and related fields into their own school makes it likely that UMDNJ's vulnerabilities, arising from its particular hierarchical structure and its culture of deference, would continue. At the same time, the dominance of medicine within research universities compared to other fields suggests that RBHS may come to exert an outsize influence on how Rutgers is governed. A similar effect from Rowan's takeover of SOM may be less likely, given that Rowan had begun its own medical school prior to that event.

The need for fiscal accountability within UMDNJ had been a theme in the Steering Committee (2004) report but the situation at Rutgers had also been a concern. The State Commission of Investigation (2007) complained of the latter's inefficient and poorly supervised budgetary and spending procedures, lax governance, and questionable expenditures on lobbying the State government. In other words, Rutgers too suffered from some distortions in its hierarchical structure.

Anticipating its needs for strong leadership during the merger, Rutgers hired a new president, Robert Barchi. His prior presidency at Thomas Jefferson Medical University was believed to qualify him to preside over the merger, although his former employer is also a freestanding health sciences university and one considerably smaller than UMDNJ.[10] Once on the job, he quickly became enmeshed in a controversy involving the athletic department, leading to questions about a "bunker style of management" (*The Record* 2013b).

If the preceding points suggest that Rutgers may not be fully equipped to deal with the negative effects of UMDNJ's hierarchical structure, there are other features of Rutgers that could be mitigating. Rutgers is a comprehensive research university with strong traditions, including independent departments in the basic sciences that could influence those fields within the RBHS. It has a history of faculty self-governance through a well-established senate, an important model for those accustomed to either the absence of or the recently reconstituted senate at UMDNJ. It has demonstrated a willingness to look outside its own borders in hiring faculty and administrators, in contrast with UMDNJ's inclinations to hire from within its ranks. For example, it hired Dr Brian L. Strom from the University of Pennsylvania to be chancellor of RBHS, beginning December 2013, where he will joined by Dr Nancy Cantor,

10 Dr Barchi, a medical doctor, has also been provost at the University of Pennsylvania, where he would have had experience in dealing with the complexities of a large comprehensive research university.

former president and chancellor of Syracuse University, as head of all other Newark operations.

Effects on Embeddedness

Of all forms of embeddedness, both the Steering Committee (2004: 62) and the Kean (2010) report expressed most concern about the influence of partisanship on higher education, particularly as demonstrated by UMDNJ's Board of Trustees. Rutgers provides a clear contrast, where the independence of its boards of Governors and Trustees has been critical in protecting its integrity from political interference. Unfortunately, that independence has come under challenge directly as a result of the merger negotiations (Linhorst and Alex 2013).

There may also be salutary effects from Rutgers naming Ted Brown as senior vice president in charge of a newly created office of enterprise risk, compliance and ethics, with the mandate to look for potential trouble (Alex 2013). Brown, who had been hired at UMDNJ in 2005 as the compliance attorney, also became its interim senior vice president and general counsel,

Effects on Dependency

UMDNJ's problems with dependency had both internal and external sources. Internally, dependency led to competition among campuses, schools, and departments, a condition of concern to the Steering Committee (2004: 56). By continuing the separation of the various schools, in particular, NJMS and RWJMS, the merger legislation perpetuated the historic boundaries between the two medical schools, each now headed by the same deans that held those offices in UMDNJ. In addition, the legislation left intact Rutgers College of Nursing, with campuses in Newark and Camden, and UMDNJ's School of Nursing in Newark, each under its existing dean. These independent operations are likely to be sources of internal competition and the longer they continue in their current form, the more difficult it will be to alter their governance.

A major source of problem at UMDNJ had been its relations with University Hospital and the uncontrollable costs those entailed. The merger removed University Hospital as a direct financial liability and, with it, the incentive to find questionable remedies to financial problems. But new problems may arise from the financial strains related to the cost of the merger itself, creating an atmosphere where the new schools are viewed as burdensome additions. Already, reactions from Rutgers faculty have been provoked from surprise at the size of some physicians' income, even though most of that income does not come from the University's budget (Alex 2014). The anticipated effects on Rowan should be more manageable since they were of less magnitude.

The merged university continues its dependence on external sources of funding. In light of this, or perhaps because of it, Dr Bachi's ties with the corporate world aroused little concern. He was hired despite informing the Board of Governors that he was on the board of two companies that did substantial business with Rutgers, one a distributor of lab supplies and the other a pharmaceutical research company (Boburg and Alex 2013; Weinberg 2013). The dependence of higher education on corporate sources of funding has a lengthy history[11] and Rutgers' corporate ties can only be expected to grow in a climate where aiding economic development is a principal goal of higher education.

The effects of the merger are still unknown. The new structures, although embedded in Rutgers, suggest some level of continuity with what previously existed at UMDNJ. In the short run, at least, that continuity will be augmented by the presence of most of the previous administrators and faculty. Nor are there clear signs that the intrusion of political interests will be barred. Even less likely is the possibility of an effective firewall against the influence of corporate interests. Judging from the time of writing, it appears that Rutgers may provide an ambiguous model for ensuring that the remnants of UMDNJ will be incorporated in ways that will lessen their vulnerability to corruption.

11 Long-time Rutgers faculty member William Vesterman (2013) offers a biting critique of the new president along with a reminder that the links between higher education and big business have a long history in the US.

CHAPTER 7

How the Education of Health Care Professionals Became Corrupted

Explaining How UMDNJ Became a "School for Scandal"

Sources of Vulnerability

UMDNJ, though it may have been unique in the timing, variety, and volume of its misconduct, can still be treated as an exemplary, even if extreme, case of how US higher education affecting the training of health care professionals became corrupted. Such treatment is justified on the grounds that most institutions of higher education were subject to similar pressures. The latter arose from major social changes resulting in a new emphasis on academic organizations as hierarchically organized corporate enterprises, accountable to external stakeholders, and under constant pressure to increase resources. Rewards are now distributed to favor administrators and those faculty who excel at garnering resources, whether ones of money, power, or prestige. Medical schools, in addition, have had to deal with the prominence accorded to biomedical research and a subsequent diminishment in the importance attached to teaching and patient care. Hospitals that are a critical component in the training of health care professionals have become an overwhelming financial burden to the universities to which they are attached. At the same time, pharmaceutical and medical device manufacturers have found medical schools an important venue in which to establish their own credentials and build a clientele for their products. However, their activities often present a challenge to norms of academic autonomy, professional ethics, and even scientific integrity. All these changes have been accompanied by an increased role for government at all levels, even in private universities. The resources that flow from government and the accountability then entailed create conditions fostering distortions in how universities report their activities. The cumulative effect of these pressures has made higher education vulnerable to corruption.

Corruption, defined as possibly illegal but always unfair and untrustworthy financial, political, and ethically-compromised actions performed by those in positions of authority, can become systemic, affecting organizations' functioning and relations among participants. Although corruption may be manifested as the search for personal advantage by organizational actors, my larger concern is with how advantage is sought for the organization itself. When the two occur in the same organization, as they did in UMDNJ, they feed off each other, reinforcing an atmosphere of rule-bending and increasing the incidence of misconduct.[1]

The argument that vulnerability to corruption in higher education has increased (e.g., Heyneman 2013; Shaw 2013; Turk 2008; Washburn 2005) may suggest an undifferentiated indictment of the whole field. Rather, vulnerability is variable, depending on the extent of pressures under which organizations operate and the opportunities that exist to enable corruption (e.g. Baucus 1994). The commonsense inference is that, the greater the vulnerability, the higher the probability that corrupt actions will follow. Even without any way of establishing statistical probabilities, it is possible to conclude from the experiences of UMDNJ that the multiple and severe pressures under which it operated were cumulative in moving it toward corruption. Similar assumptions can then be made about comparable universities.

Chapter 3 relied on the organizational literature to derive a series of hypotheses about the relation between organizational characteristics under conditions of vulnerability and either the incentives encouraging corruption or the opportunities available for its expression. All the expected relationships were supported by data from UMDNJ in the two chapters that followed. In addition, examination of UMDNJ's core and network organization uncovered three pathways that led to actual misconduct. One, located in the core, stemmed from distortions in its hierarchical system. The second, located in the network, originated from its embedded relations. The third, common to both the core and the network, derived from its dependency. Although those pathways emerged from the data in ways that were not directly anticipated, they converge with the hypothesized relationships to form a more concise way of conceptualizing the road to corruption. Their main contours are reiterated here to emphasize the processes through which they arose and their general relevance to corruption in higher education.

Hierarchical Distortions

The prototypic bureaucratic organization is made up of offices arranged in tiers, where skill levels and degrees of authority increase as one moves up the hierarchy. Lines of command are clear, with orders flowing downward and information upward. Authority is legitimate insofar as it is achieved according to accepted principles of technical qualification for the job. Authority retains

---

1 Although Pinto et al. (2008) consider corrupt organizations and organizations of corrupt individuals to be two distinct types of organization-level corruption, my concern with corrupt organizations necessarily includes the behavior of corrupt individuals.

its legitimacy through impartiality in following rules binding on all who are part of the organization.

Popular discontent with bureaucratic organization is often expressed through complaints about red tape and inflexibility in applying rules. Moreover, the impersonal manner of the bureaucrat may be interpreted as lack of concern for those being served. Although such complaints may signal genuine impediments to the efficient operation of a bureaucratic organization, in themselves, they do not reflect the kinds of distortions that lead to serious misconduct. Instead, within UMDNJ, critical distortions arose from an over-reliance on hierarchical structures in almost all significant arenas, overriding alternative organizational forms that foster cooperation and collegiality. Hierarchical arrangements were favored by administrators because they gave them the control needed to provide some order over multiple campuses, schools, and services and present a unified face in dealing with external stakeholders. All this went in hand with a lack of transparency on how decisions were made.

Some consequences of hierarchy at UMDNJ, like depressing collaboration across departments, schools, and campuses, had no direct effect on corruption. However, by contributing to an insular climate, they did strengthen the likelihood of structural holes. Those holes, in turn, led to asymmetries in information that could be exploited for unfair advantage (Burt 1992; Prechel and Morris 2010: 335). Existing forms of hierarchy allowed administrators to accumulate resources of money and power that they could use at their discretion and be free of restraining rules. With hierarchy the overarching model both for the University as a whole and its subunits, combined with a culture of deference associated with the dominance of medicine, the result was an unwillingness to express criticisms, reinforced by administrators' power to punish critics.

Embeddedness

Institutional embeddedness refers to the ways organizations are linked to each other. It may take the form of market embeddedness, in which transitory and impersonal relations typically characterize contacts like buying and selling. In contrast, it may be a feature of network relations, in which there are continuing ties of obligation (Granovetter 2007). Or it may describe relations with the state, involving oversight and regulation, generally of a continuing nature (Prechel 2000). Just as the hierarchical structure of organizations can be understood to have both positive and negative effects, the same is true for embeddedness. Institutional embeddedness may lead to relations built on trust and fairness or they can promote rent-seeking and exploitation (Granovetter 1985: 493; Prechel 2000).

The negative side of embeddedness for UMDNJ appeared in all three kinds of relations through discretionary methods for assigning unfair benefits. Market relations were distorted when the University issued contracts without following requirements for public bidding and contacts with vendors were stabilized through gift-giving. In general, market relations that should have been based on trust were treated instrumentally, in the search for advantage. Obligations to sustain network relations were converted to illegal and unethical modes through adding unfair benefits and suppressing criticism. Political embeddedness, an outgrowth of its dependence on the state of New Jersey for its functioning and existence, the federal government for funding and regulation, and local governments for creating favorable environments, was corrupted through cronyism and the subversion of unbiased ways of assigning benefits.

Dependency

Resource dependency (Pfeffer and Salancik 1978) was the most critical characteristic of UMDNJ, both within its core and in its network relations. The unending search for resources of money, power, and status and the constant uncertainty about their acquisition defined UMDNJ's vulnerability. Dependency was a powerful incentive to ensure and increase resources in whatever manner and from whatever source seemed likely (Tenbrunsel 1998). It was associated with competitive pressures to gain advantage that, tied to geographic and structural divisions within the University, reduced potential collegiality, encouraged gaming the system, and stimulated the search for whatever means, regardless of legality or adherence to ethical standards, would reduce dependency.

Within the core organization, dependency led to self-protective efforts on the part of individuals, departments, and schools to buffer their primary activities against competing demands from others in the University. The result was another means to diminish collegiality and block internal transparency. Relations with network partners were dominated by efforts to reduce dependency and, while using the full array of bridging strategies, favored coopting those politicians willing to enter into quid pro quo relations. Cooptation was used as well with community groups and their leaders. Oversight and rating agencies that could not be dealt with through cooptation received, instead, misleading information, some of which was tied to overtly illegal behavior.

General Relevance

The theoretical underpinnings for explaining organizational corruption were presented in Chapter 3 through a series of hypotheses derived from the literature on organizations. Those hypotheses, in turn, were the means to anticipate finding presented in Chapters 4 and 5. The three principal characteristics defined as the pathways to corruption were not, in themselves, anticipated but emerged from the findings. They are not, however, competitors to the hypotheses. The hypotheses were geared to processes; the findings are characterisitcs that subsume the processes.

Hierarchy, embeddedness, and dependency were not exclusive characteristics of UMDNJ but describe the structures of higher education generally. Analysis of UMDNJ reveals how these attributes may have a negative side and how that negativity is critical to creating and sustaining systemic corruption. We learn from UMDNJ that the corrupting influences resulting from hierarchy stem from a lack of transparency, administrative discretion, norms of deference, and the absence of countervailing organizational forms. Corrupting influences from embeddedness arise when relations, whether taking place in an impersonal and transitory market, in networks of obligation, or in the political realm, can be manipulated through discretionary actions alert to obtaining unfair advantage. Dependency can produce a powerful push to corruption when needs for resources are great and uncertainty is high. Then there is a premium on blocking transparency, buffering core operations, and coopting those with resources.

By tracing the origins and outcomes of these conditions at UMDNJ and their tie to its misconduct, we are left with a virtual prototype of how the corruption of academic medical centers may take place. The following section explores this further by considering how UMDNJ was similar to other institutions of higher education.

UMDNJ as an Exemplar of Global Corruption

Transparency International's 2013 *Global Corruption Report,* devoted to education, covers results from a broad spectrum of countries, from the richest and most developed to the poorest and least developed. In assessing corruption in higher education based on those data, Heyneman (2013) presents risk factors and possible solutions in ways that demonstrate the larger significance of UMDNJ's experiences. Just as I have located the roots of UMDNJ's problems in its resource dependency and its limited competitive ability, he generalizes that "Competition for resources, fame and notoriety place extraordinary pressures on higher education institutions. The weaker ones, those with an absence of control or managerial strength, are most prone to corruption" (Heyneman 2013: 101).

Lack of transparency was an important means by which UMDNJ could engage in illegal and unethical behavior for long periods without detection. It fostered insulated hierarchies of authority with discretionary powers, promoted ways of evading regulations, and encouraged unfairness in how rewards were distributed. Heyneman (2013: 103) contrasts this with the positive effects of transparency.

> While access to information cannot guarantee a reduction of corruption nor provide significant empowerment of the public, it can be 'an effective tool for claiming other rights' and establishing accountability structures. The *Global Corruption Report* assesses the possibility that higher education corruption could be reduced if universities were more transparent about their internal decision-making.

The *Global Corruption Report* emphasizes how good university governance can counter tendencies to corruption. Such governance is manifested through the quality of the education provided, honesty in how financial resources are used, the selection of faculty and administrators through open competition, and supervision by autonomous boards (Heyneman 2013: 103–104). In contrast, UMDNJ's governance was compromised by a lax and politicized Board of Trustees, inward-looking criteria in the selection of administrators, and dishonest financial dealings. UMDNJ was unchallenged only by the quality of the education it provided but even that was put in jeopardy by instances of inappropriate grade changing, student cheating, pressure to admit students with incomplete credentials, and ineffective training in some residency programs.

The global review of university practices places great responsibility on the professoriate and recognizes how the competitive pressures it faces may lead to corruption. The reward system may be perceived as unfair, leading to fissures in the normative underpinnings of universities. At UMDNJ this was manifested in the contrast between administrative and faculty salaries and in questions about the fairness of rewards. Most egregious were salaries awarded as virtual bribes, as in the case of the cardiologists hired to steer patients to University Hospital or politicians hired to increase state allocations. Although the University administration bargained with a variety of unions representing faculty and staff, the latter were not able to keep abuses in check. The *Global Report* found it particularly troubling "that the power of faculty senates has eroded over time and that university managers act in an increasingly cavalier fashion, because power is now concentrated with them" (Heyneman 2013: 104). This assessment is in line with my own evaluation of how the absence of an independent faculty senate at UMDNJ had negative consequences.

Comparison of pressures on higher education globally with the experiences of UMDNJ point to a convergence in the factors leading to corruption. Rather than standing out by its uniqueness, UMDNJ now appears to have been part of a general trend undermining the integrity of higher education.

Assigning Blame

Structures vs. Actors

UMDNJ's corruption and, by extension, the corruption of higher education generally, originated from the environmental and structural pressures that open organizations to deviance. Those pressures were experienced as incentives to reach and enhance organizational goals by searching for greater opportunities for their achievement, even when these involve illegal or unethical means. Like all repeated activities, the illegal and unethical also became institutionalized and the normative culture that evolved helped justify continuing misconduct.

Organizations act only through the agency of specific actors, which raises the question of why it would not be preferable to examine these actors individually and determine why they make the choices they do. In the case of UMDNJ, preceding chapters have singled out many such actors involved in questionable behavior. Most held administrative positions, beginning with presidents and including vice presidents, deans, and department chairs. Others were staff in administrative offices, like those dealing with legal affairs or billing. Those singled out in the network included elected officeholders and members of the Board of Trustees. Questions were also raised about the impartiality of those who served on University or University-related committees whose primary affiliation were with pharmaceutical manufacturers or other New Jersey-based businesses. The role of administrators and their staff in UMDNJ's corruption was anticipated in Chapter 3, where it was hypothesized that "management sets the stage for organizational misconduct." Administrators' actions and those they stimulated their staff to carry out were primarily aimed at benefitting the University.[2] The remaining actors, mainly found in the network, acted solely to benefit themselves. These differences illustrate the importance of the locale in uncovering where the two types of organizational-level corruption may predominate (Pinto et al. 2008).

2 Administrators also received personal benefits, especially in the form of perks. In addition, they could anticipate indirect benefits that would flow from their role in enhancing the University's prestige.

Isolating more precise characteristics of individual wrongdoers is more difficult, particularly given the kind of data available for this analysis. Baucus, out of ten hypotheses in her model of corporate illegality, was able to come up with only a single one predicting individual behavior: *"Individuals with an external locus of control, or operating at a fairly low level of moral reasoning, or exhibiting Machiavellian tendencies likely engage in intentional illegality"* (Baucus 1994: 715). [Emphasis in the original] Not only does testing Baucus's hypothesis require access to psychological measures of personality but her language refers specifically to intentional behavior. In effect, she is acknowledging that, in many instances, unethical behavior is tied to self-deceptions rather than to a conscious sense of wrongdoing (see also Tensbrunsel and Messick 2004). As other researchers have discovered (e.g. Benson 1985; Vaughan 1996), there are deep-seated tendencies to rationalize rule-bending or rule-breaking behavior, leading to the normalization of deviance, especially when it validates an ethic where the end justifies the means (Gray 2013: 13). For such reasons, most researchers tend to focus on the organizational roots of corruption rather than on individual perpetrators (e.g., Darley 1996; Dunn and Schweitzer 2005). Burt's (2012) recent research into the impact of individual psychological characteristics on behavior in networks (in which what I have called the core organization is also understood as a network of relations) concludes that, while they are relevant, it is difficult to establish their effects. I take from his research the importance, instead, of network location, specifically in how those who bridge structural holes, like the administrative staff was able to do at UMDNJ, have opportunities to pursue their own route to advantage.

Ways of identifying the agents responsible for leading an organization into systemic corruption remain a tantalizing task if we wish to move beyond locating the roles they occupy. But, in many instances, the knowledge gained would not add significantly to our understanding. This is because knowing the identity of major culprits is only critical to those seeking to bring indictments in a court of law. Focusing on particular individuals leads to the conclusion, as stated by the federal monitor (Stern 2008: 3), that there were only a small number of bad apples at UMDNJ who brought it into disrepute while the majority of faculty and staff were carrying out their duties responsibly. In other words, the particular individuals who participate in questionable behavior are only one aspect of a larger reality. If we want to understand the dynamics of organizational corruption, we have to look primarily at how it emerges out of an organization's structure and the ways it interacts with its environment.

Whistleblowers and Bystanders

An additional perspective on why organizational factors are so important to the emergence and continuity of organizational corruption comes from looking at those individuals who decide to make public the misconduct they witness. Such whistleblowers are protected by law in the United States and are even described as heroes in the popular media. But, in the workplace, they are often met with contempt for their disloyalty, viewed as informers, and even ostracized (Johnson 2003: 26–28). Given how the organizational environment frequently discourages speaking out, whistleblowers are, in fact, unusual. At UMDNJ, some personnel did avail themselves of the confidential phone and email lines that the federal monitor set up to receive complaints[3] and their names were redacted. But there were few known whistleblowers plus a number of others who sued the University or its components because they had been fired or otherwise punished for complaining about corrupt practices. Willingly or not, all of the latter left the University.

Kenny's (2013) study of whistleblowers was based on those in banking organizations where, in general, externally-imposed regulations were disparaged and those in charge of compliance were disrespected. In a strongly hierarchical structure, compliance officers were located at a relatively low level. Within this context, she goes on to identify two features that militate against participants exposing misconduct. The first is "deafened ears," a result that follows where "there is little support from one's colleagues who operate amid fears of being singled out themselves, losing their jobs and compromising their and the families' well-being." Consequently, "It is futile to speak where no audience is listening." In the environments studied, "huge obstacles are in place that would prevent others in the organization from even hearing about problems." The second obstacle is "incentivised silence," where those speaking out report to managers who are themselves seriously compromised. The latter "operate in a culture that significantly incentivises their silence, both from their place in the bank's hierarchy and the desire to 'keep the directors happy,' but also from the fact that they stand to receive generous compensation in return for *not* upsetting the status quo."

Kenny's work carries over to more general insights into why whistleblowing remains a relatively infrequent means for dealing with organizational corruption. It concludes, as I have done in the case of UMDNJ, that organizational misconduct continues due to hierarchical structures that discourage

3 Between January and July 2006, the hotline received 124 emails and 95 telephone calls (Stern 2006: 39).

transparency and to the allocation of rewards to those with an unquestioning orientation toward the organization's well-being. Where regulations are seen as an impediment to organizational achievements, a culture emerges that permits, if not encourages, their side-stepping. Those prepared to question these premises are, within the culture that legitimizes their organization, defined as inadequately committed to the organization and disloyal to their colleagues.

These findings also shed light on an unanticipated problem encountered in the conduct of the present research. The latter is based on reports of the federal monitor; other government and court documents; newspaper reports, especially from investigative reporters; and interviews with past and present employees or persons knowledgeable about UMDNJ. It was the last source of data that proved difficult to obtain. Although I have extensive experience in conducting interviews of all kinds, including with those who questioned my intentions and the purpose of my research, and even assumed an ideological conflict with me, my experience in studying UMDNJ was unique. In recruiting persons to interview, I assured them that I was doing an academic study of how the university worked. Because I already had access to all the public records of misconduct, I had no reason to look for more. I would also assure them of their anonymity. At times I made contacts through intermediaries who would vouch for my credentials. Yet many of those contacted would not even return phone calls or emails. Altogether, compared to past experience, I received an unusual number of refusals. Research on whistleblowers provides some answers for why this happened.

From those employed at UMDNJ, whether or not they allowed themselves to be interviewed, I heard that the University had been unfairly maligned. The following reasons were given to justify that view:

> Whatever wrongdoing had been uncovered could be blamed on a small group of administrators.
>
> When misconduct occurred, it was concentrated in only a few locales, like University Hospital in Newark or the School of Osteopathic Medicine in Camden.
>
> Constant attention from journalists only served to undermine all the good the University accomplished.
>
> Faculty and most staff members were conscientious in fulfilling their obligations to students and patients.
>
> There had already been too much focus on what had gone wrong and it was time to allow the University to move out of the spotlight and perform the activities it was qualified to carry out.

All these sentiments were, to a degree, understandable, although not all were factually correct. When stated directly to me, they evoked my sympathy even as I tried to persuade the speaker to participate in my research.

But what is the appropriate response to such bystanders? Were they, in fact, totally unaware of what had been occurring? Had they, by their silence, been in complicity with the University's corruption? Did their continuing silence mean they were still unwilling to come to terms with the structural roots of what had gone wrong? My role as an independent researcher makes it inappropriate to moralize about why individuals choose not to participate in a study. At the same time, their behavior is a critical indicator of why corruption is able to be sustained alongside normal organizational behavior. It is not because there are a few bad apples, to be eventually found out, but because of an existing structure and culture that promotes the pursuit of organizational goals through both legitimate and illegal and unethical means. Only through uncovering those structural roots and the interactions they foster can we begin to understand why organizational corruption emerges and persists.

Lessons from UMDNJ

This review has pointed to numerous parallels in the experience of corruption at UMDNJ with other institutions of higher education globally. These parallels held even though UMDNJ was distinctive as a free-standing, state-supported university solely devoted to the health care professions. They led me to propose that, since all of higher education had become vulnerable to corruption as a result of similar pressures, the pathways from vulnerability to misconduct followed by UMDNJ would be more generally applicable. That is, other corrupt institutions could be anticipated to have made similar responses to dependency and embeddedness and adopted comparable modes of hierarchy. This was the sense in which UMDNJ was an exemplar. Moving beyond UMDNJ's unique history, organizational make-up, and state and local environments, we can find many ways in which it provides general lessons about the dangers waiting when universities respond to their vulnerabilities. Whether or not those lessons offer practical guidelines to faculty and administrators will be a test of the potential for organizational change.

Within the confines of hierarchy, UMDNJ demonstrated the pitfalls of administrative control coupled with lack of transparency. What it needed were alternative structures that encourage faculty input and participation in administrative decisions. The desirability of such changes is premised on faculty having professional commitments and networks that expose them to alternative perspectives and support them in the pursuit of scholarly goals. Faculty can then affirm the importance of scholarship, teaching, and service that adheres to professional standards when dealing with administrators, secure in the knowledge that they have the backing of their organized peers. But for professional values to be an effective counter to corrupting influences, it is essential that the varied professional groups that make up a modern university be prepared to overcome disciplinary biases and work toward common collegial goals. In essence, this means that medicine must be prepared to relax its demands for deference. While excessive attachment to professional values has its own dangers, those values still provide a useful antidote to an enveloping organization-specific identity.

Of the three kinds of embeddedness that provided UMDNJ with opportunities for corruption, the one involving markets is potentially the easiest to repair. Misconduct could be minimized through clear regulations monitored internally, by compliance officers who work transparently and with full support from the administration and externally, by state oversight. Although some kinds of relevant legislation already existed in New Jersey, for example, on bidding for contracts, UMDNJ had found oversight relatively easy to evade. The state subsequently added further regulation and, in the last years of its existence, UMDNJ hired and empowered compliance personnel.

UMDNJ's experiences with embeddedness in network and political relations point to greater difficulty in controlling the potential for corruption from these sources. Only ties with professional accrediting and status-conferring agencies proved insulated from inappropriate efforts at influence. In contrast, relations with New Jersey government and its oversight agencies, in particular, its Board of Trustees, demonstrated the ease with which UMDNJ's borders could be penetrated, and mirroring this, the ease with which UMDNJ could mislead its governmental overseers. Those outcomes argue for the importance of independent, well-qualified, and attentive boards and the cultivation of arm's length relations between states and their universities. Most troubling of all were relations with those in surrounding communities. The latter, directly affected by a university's operations, deserve a respectful hearing without either party to the relationship becoming subject to coercive pressures. How that can be achieved is essential to discover but beyond the scope of this study.

For most universities in the U.S., there are few alternatives to reliance on the external environment for resources, whether of money, power, or status. With continually rising costs, even vast endowments have become inadequate to shield universities from the need for additional money. In UMDNJ's case, it was constrained by its existence as a state agency, its limited access to independent sources of funding, and the requirement that it provide health care services to large numbers of uninsured patients, with the latter an especially burdensome drain on the University's financial well-being. Given that its hospital ties were the most critical factor in its financial corruption, UMDNJ demonstrated the necessity for finding other ways of funding hospital-based training of students and alternate ways for universities to engage in relations with hospitals. This is a well-recognized problem (Ginzberg 1996), made more acute by the untenable cost structures currently associated with hospital administration generally.

The heightened prominence of biomedical research has intensified competition for the status that success in these fields brings, raising the likelihood of fraud by researchers (Fang et al. 2012) and undue influence from corporate sponsors (Brennan et al. 2006), coupled with the reluctance of universities to punish wrongdoers (e.g. Luthra). Even when none of these negative outcomes surface, the search for scientific success brings universities into uncomfortable contact with the commercial world (Dupree 2008). In the case of UMDNJ, raising its status through the achievements of individual researchers was difficult because the latter were themselves affected by UMDNJ's comparative ranking among other universities. If its experiences, consequently, do not provide much guidance, they are still a reminder of how important it is to hold academic research to the highest scientific standards while insulating it from excessive external pressures.

Power is a resource that can follow from money or status but its primary roots are associated with organizational position. Power can become corrupted, as it did at UMDNJ, when it is used arbitrarily to confer unfair advantages. Along with using power internally to control actors and activities, universities search for political resources to reduce dependency from intrusion by external interests. This form of dependency then overlaps with the political embeddedness that links the two. The search for protective political influence easily moves into troublesome partisan terrain. Some, if not most, of UMDNJ's political problems could have been avoided if there had been firmer barriers between it and its political milieu. Although the state must provide needed oversight, it could do so by removing the latter from the possibility of partisan or personal advantage. Even a state as politicized as New Jersey could accomplish this under committed political leadership.

The UMDNJ described in these pages no longer exists. Its disappearance as a free-standing university leaves behind a series of lessons about the effects of organizational structures and decisions and the environment in which they operate. As the remnants of the original find their place in Rutgers and Rowan Universities, we wish them insight into what went wrong in the past and wisdom to deal with the pressures that will continue to make them vulnerable to misconduct.

References[1]

AAUP-UMDNJ. http://www.aaupumdnj.org.

ACGME. 2007. *ACGME Institutional Requirements*. http://www.acgme.org/acWebsite/newsRoom.

Alex, Patricia. 2012a. "School's Exclusion of SAT Data May Violate Ethics." *The Record* (March 16).

——. 2012b. "SAT Data Fails Test." *The Record* (March 15).

——. 2012c. "UMDNJ Settles Bias Suit for $4.6M." *The Record* (December 8).

——. 2013. "Risk Chief Seeks Team Effort." *The Record* (December 6).

——. 2014. "Income Puts Rutgers Doctors among Elite." *The Record* (March 18).

Altbach Philip G. 2011. "Patterns of Higher Education Development." In *American Higher Education in the Twenty-First Century: Social, Political, and Economic Challenges*, edited by Philip G. Altbach, Patricia J. Gumport, and Robert O. Berdahl, 15–36. 3rd ed. Baltimore, MD: Johns Hopkins University Press.

Amirault, Ben. 2009. "Double-Billing Settlement Highlights Whistleblower Concerns." *HealthLeaders Media* (June 12). http://www.healthleadersmedia.com/pront/FIN-234437/Doublebilling-.

Austad, Kirsten E. and Aaron S. Kesselheim. 2011. "Conflict of Interest Disclosure in Early Education of Medical Students." *JAMA* 306(9): 991–992.

Barer, Sol J. 2012. *The University of Medicine and Dentistry of New Jersey Advisory Committee*. Final Report. Trenton, NJ: State of New Jersey.

Basken, Paul. 2013. "UCLA, Eyeing Profits, Entrusts Tech Transfer to Industry Experts." *Chronicle of Higher Education* (August 12).

Baucus, Melissa S. 1994. "Pressure, Opportunity and Predisposition: A Multivariate Model of Corporate Illegality." *Journal of Management* 20(4): 699–721.

Benson, M. 1985. "Denying the Guilty Mind: Accounting for Involvement in a White-Collar Crime." *Criminology* 23 (November): 583–607.

Bentham, Jeremy. 1999. In *Political Tactics*, edited by M. James, C. Blamires, and C. Pease-Watkin. Oxford: Oxford University Press.

Berman, Elizabeth Popp. 2011. *Creating the Market University: How Academic Science Became an Economic Engine*. Princeton: Princeton University Press.

Birnbaum, Robert. 1988. *How Colleges Work: The Cybernetics of Academic Organization and Leadership*. San Francisco, CA: Jossey-Bass.

1 All the websites relating to UMDNJ have been taken down since its dissolution and mergers. They will be available as paper copies, along with all the newspaper articles, in the special collections archive of UMDNJ at Rutgers University.

Blauner, Bob. 2009. *Resisting McCarthyism: To Sign or Not to Sign California's Loyalty Oath*. Stanford, CA: Stanford University Press.

Block, Alan A. 1996. "American Corruption and the Decline of the Progressive Ethos." *Journal of Law and Society* 23 (March): 18–35.

Boburg, Shawn and Patricia Alex. 2013. "Barchi Has Links with Firms Paid by Rutgers." *The Record* (July 15).

Bok, Derek. 2004. *Universities in the Marketplace: The Commercialization of Higher Education*. Princeton, NJ: Princeton University Press.

Boozang, Kathleen M. 2007–2008. "Does an Independent Board Improve Nonprofit Corporate Governance?" *Tennessee Law Review* 75: 83–136.

Braun, Robert J. 1994. "UMDNJ Donation Fuels Fire on Higher Ed." *Star-Ledger* (April 6).

——. 2004. "The Doctor Declined to Open Wide and Say 'Ugh!'." *Star-Ledger* (April 21).

Brennan, Troyen A., David J. Rothman, Linda Blank, David Blumenthal, Susan C. Chimonas, Jordan J. Cohen, Janlori Goldman, Jerome P. Kassirer, Harry Kimball, James Naughton, and Neil Smelser. 2006. "Health Industry Practices That Create Conflicts of Interest: A Policy Proposal for Academic Medical Centers." *Journal of the American Medical Association* 295(4): 429–433.

Burt, Ronald. 1992. *Structural Holes*. Cambridge, MA: Harvard University Press.

Burt, Ronald S. 2012. "Network-Related Personality and the Agency Question: Multirole Evidence from a Virtual World." *American Journal of Sociology* 118 (November): 543–591.

Campbell, Carol Ann. 1998. "UMDNJ Passes the Reins to Insider – Acting Chief Cook Will Succeed Bergen." *Star Ledger* (November 24).

——. 2002a. "UMDNJ's Autonomy Is at Risk – State Panel to Study Merger with Rutgers." *Star-Ledger* (March 6).

——. 2002b. "Patchwork of UMDNJ Schools Examined – Top Goal of McGreevey Panel Is to Create a Uniform Health Education System." *Star-Ledger* (March 7).

——. 2005. "Scientists Win a Reprieve from Eviction – UMDNJ Still Seeks Back Rent for Newark Site." *Star Ledger* (January 12).

Campbell, Carol Ann and Bev McCarron. 2002. "UMDNJ Leadership Opposes a Merger – Strongly Faults Plan to Join Rutgers, NJIT." *Star-Ledger* (November 9).

Campbell, Carol Ann and Angela Stewart. 2002. "Lawmakers in Essex Resist College Merger – Rutgers-UMDNJ Union Focus of Hearings." *Star-Ledger* (September 17).

Carney, Leo. 2005. "Critical Condition: Charges of Medical Fraud, Office-Break-Ins, Political Patronage, and Criminal Probes Have the University of Medicine and Dentistry of New Jersey on Life Support." *New Jersey Monthly* (November). Posted February 8, 2008. http://njmonthly.com/articles/lifestyle/people/critical-conditions.html.

Chen, David W. 2006. "With a New Jersey University under Federal Oversight, Corzine Removes Its President." *New York Times* (January 23).

Christie, Christopher. 2010. *Executive Order 26*. Office of the Governor. Trenton, NJ: State of New Jersey.

Cluff, Leighton E. 1983. "Economic Incentives of Faculty Practice: Are They Distorting the Medical School's Mission?" *Journal of the American Medical Association* 250 (December 2): 2931–2934.

Cohen, Linda R. 1998. "Soft Money, Hard Choices: Research Universities and University Hospitals." In *Challenges to Research Universities*, edited by Roger G. Noll, 147–169. Washington, DC: Brookings Institution Press.

Cohen, Linda R. and Roger G. Noll. 1998. "Universities, Constituencies, and the Role of the States." In *Challenges to Research Universities*, edited by Roger G. Noll, 31–62. Washington, DC: Brookings Institution Press.

Cohen, M.D. and J.G. March. 1986. "Leadership in an Organized Anarchy." In *Organization and Governance in Higher Education*, edited by M.C. Brown, II, 16–35. Boston, MA: Pearson Custom Publishing.

Cohen, Wesley M., Richard Florida, Lucien Randazzese, and John Walsh. 1998. "Industry and the Academy: Uneasy Partners in the Cause of Technological Advance." In *Challenges to Research Universities*, edited by Roger G. Noll, 171–199. Washington, DC: Brookings Institution Press.

Cole, Jonathan. 2010. *The Great American University: Its Rise to Preeminence, Its Indispensable National Role, Why it Must Be Protected.* New York: Public Affairs.

Commission on Health Science, Education, and Training. 2004. *The Report of the New Jersey Commission on Health Science, Education, and Training* (Vagelos Report). Trenton, NJ.

Conrad, Peter. 1988. "Learning to Doctor: Reflections on Recent Accounts of the Medical School Years." *Journal of Health and Social Behavior* 29 (December): 323–332.

Corbett, Nic and Jenna Portnoy. 2012. "Dramatic Restructuring of N.J.'s University System Would Create 3 Research Campuses." *Star-Ledger* (January 26).

Corporate Crime, Reporter. 2004. "Public Corruption in the United States." Washington, DC: September 16.

Cosgrove, Lisa, Harold J. Bursztajn, Sheldon Krimsky, Maria Anaya, and Justin Walker. 2009. "Conflicts of Interest and Disclosure in the American Psychiatric Association's Clinical Practice Guidelines." *Journal of Psychotherapy and Psychosomatics* 78(4): 228–232.

Coughlin, Kevin. 2004. "UMDNJ Faces a Suit from a Prized Tenant - Health Institute Says School Broke Promises." *Star Ledger* (December 23).

Curcio, Diane. 1989. "Attorney Sues School Over Firing." *Star-Ledger* (October 15).

CWA 1031. http://www.cwa1031.org.

Darley, John M. 1996. "How Organizations Socialize Individuals into Evildoing." In *Codes of Conduct: Behavior Research into Business Ethics*, edited by D.M. Messick and A.E. Tenbrunsel, 13–42. New York: Russell Sage Foundation.

Deferred Prosecution Agreement. 2005. Office of the United States Attorney. District of New Jersey. December 30.

della Porta, Donatella and Alberto Vannucci. 1999. *Corrupt Exchanges: Actors, Resources, and Mechanisms of Political Corruption*. Hawthorne, NY: Aldine de Gruyter.

Department of Justice. 2009. "New Jersey University Hospital to Pay Additional $2 Million to Resolve Fraud Claims that Facility Double Billed Medicaid." *Office of Public Affairs*. Washington, DC: (June 9). http://www.justice.gov/print/PrintOut3.jsp.

Dincer, Oguzhan C. and Burak Gunalp. 2005. "Corruption, Income Inequality and Growth: Evidence from U.S. States." Working Paper Series. http://ssm.com.

Dobel, J. Patrick. 1978. "The Corruption of a State." *American Political Science Review* 72 (September): 958–973.

Dowling, Matthew J. 2004. "Architect of Merger Quits Posts – Former CEO of Merck Admits Rutgers Failure." *Star-Ledger* (April 5).

Dunn, Jennifer and Maurice E. Schweitzer. 2005. "Why Good Employees Make Unethical Decisions: The Role of Reward Systems, Organizational Culture, and Managerial Oversight." In *Managing Organizational Deviance*, edited by Roland E. Kidwell, Jr. and Christopher L. Martin, 39–60. Thousand Oaks, CA: Sage.

Dupree, Janet Rae. 2008. "When Academia Puts Profit Ahead of Wonder." *New York Times* (September 7).

Editorial. 1999. "The Wrong Name." *Star-Ledger* (September 28).

——. 2005. "An Ailing Medical School." *Star Ledger* (July 23).

Ehrenberg, Ronald G. 2000. *Tuition Rising: Why College Costs so Much*. Cambridge, MA: Harvard University Press.

——. 2003. "Method or Madness? Inside the *USNWR* College Rankings." CHERI Working Paper #39. Retrieved August 3 2012 from Cornell University, ILR School site: http://digitalcommons.ilr.cornell.edu/working papers/42/.

Ekel Peter D. and Adrianna Kazar. 2006. "The Challenges Facing Academic Decision Making: Contemporary Issues and Steadfast Structures." In *The Shifting Frontiers of Academic Decision Making*, edited by Peter D. Ekel, 1–14. Westport, CT: Praeger Publishers.

Elazar, Daniel J. 1972. *American Federalism: A View from the States*. New York: Thomas Y. Crowell.

Epstein, Sue. 2004. "Lacy Leaving Jersey's Top Health Post to Run Hospital – Cardiologist Will Head Robert Wood Johnson Medical Facility." *Star-Ledger* (December 3).

Fang, Ferric C., R. Grant Steen, and Arturo Casadeval. 2012. "Misconduct Accounts for the Majority of Retracted Scientific Publications." *PNAS, Proceedings of the National Academy of Sciences*. dx.doi.org/10.1073/pnas.12297109(2012).

Fennell, Mary L. and Crystal M. Adams. 2011. "U.S. Health-Care Organizations: Complexity, Turbulence, and Multilevel Change." *Annual Review of Sociology* 37: 205–219.

Fincher, Cameron. 2003. *Historical Development of the University System of Georgia, 1932–2002*. 2nd ed. Athens, GA: Georgia Institute of Higher Education.

Fischman, Josh and staff of U.S. News and World Report. 2008. *U.S. News Ultimate Guide to Medical Schools*. 3rd ed. Naperville, IL: Sourcebooks Inc.

Fisher, Marla Jo. 2006. "M.D. Says UCI Fired Him For Speaking Up." *Orange County Register* (February 3).

Fisher, Robin Gaby. 1998. "Bergen Era Ends-Father of UMDNJ Lets Go of His Obsession." *Star Ledger* (June 7).

Flexner, Abraham. 1910. *Medical Education in the United States and Canada*. Report to the Carnegie Foundation for the Advancement of Teaching. Boston: Marymount Press.

Freidson, Elliot. 1988. *Profession of Medicine: A Study of the Sociology of Applied Knowledge*. Chicago: University of Chicago Press.

——. 2006. *Professional Dominance: The Social Structure of Medical Care*. New Brunswick, NJ: Transaction Publishers.

Friedman, Alexi. 2008. "Oversight Didn't Halt Abuses at UMDNJ." *Star Ledger* (October 26).

Friedman, Matt and Kelly Heyboer, 2013 "Oliver Will Block Effort to Disband Rutgers Board." *Star-Ledger* (July 18).

Frohman, Larry, John Katz, and Emanuel Goldman. 2004. "UMDNJ Must Have Only the Best Leader." *Star Ledger* (January 30).

Gamble, Molly. 2012. "OIG Claims Georgetown University Hospital Overbilled Medicare by 659K." *Becker's Hospital Review* (April 25).

Ganem, Janice L., Robert L. Beran, and Jack K. Krakower. 1995. "Review of U.S. Medical School Finances, 1993–1994." *Journal of the American Medical Association* 274(9): 723–730.

Gettleman, Jeffrey. 2005. "Corruption? Voters Say They Know It When They See It." *New York Times* (October 17).

Ginzberg, Eli, ed. 1996. *Urban Medical Centers: Balancing Academic and Patient Care Functions*. Boulder, CO: Westview Press.

Glaeser, Edward L. and Raven E. Saks. 2004. "Corruption in America." Cambridge, MA: National Bureau of Economic Research, Working Paper Series. http://www.nber.org/paper/w10821.

Goldberger, Martin L., Brendon A. Maher, Pamela Ebert Flattau, eds. 1995. *Research Doctorate Programs in the United States: Continuity and Change*. Washington: National Academies Press.

Granovetter, Mark. 1985. "Economic Action and Social Structure: The Problem of Embeddedness." *American Journal of Sociology* 91 (November): 481–501.

Granovetter, Mark. 2007. "The Social Construction of Corruption." In *On Capitalism*, edited by Victor Nee and Richard Swedberg, 152–172. Stanford: Stanford University Press.

Gray, Garry C. 2013. "Insider Accounts of Institutional Corruption: Examining the Social Organization of Unethical Behaviour." *British Journal of Criminology* 53 (July): 533–551.

Greenberg, Daniel S. 2010. "Hubris in Grantland." *Academe* 96 (November–December): 34–38.

Greve, Henrich, Donald Palmer, and Jo-Ellen Pozner. 2010. "Organizations Gone Wild: The Causes, Processes, and Consequences of Organizational Misconduct." *Academy of Management Annals* 4(1): 53–107.

Grob, Gerald N. and Allan V. Horvitz. 2010. *Diagnoses, Therapy, and Evidence: Conundrums in Modern American Medicine*. New Brunswick, NJ: Rutgers University Press.

Hafferty, Frederic W. 1998. "Beyond Curriculum Reform: Confronting Medicine's Hidden Curriculum." *Academic Medicine* 73 (April): 403–407.

Hafferty, Frederic W. and Rondal Franks. 1994. "The Hidden Curriculum, Ethics Teaching, and the Structure of Medical Education." *Academic Medicine* 69 (November): 861–871.

Hall, Mark A., Elizabeth Dugan, Beiyao Zheng, and Aneil K. Mishra. 2001. "Trust in Physicians and Medical Institutions: What Is It, Can It Be Measured, and Does It Matter?" *The Milbank Quarterly* 79(4): 613–639.

Hamel, Gary. 2011. "First, Let's Fire All the Managers." *Harvard Business Review* 80 (December).

Hauser, Robert M. and John Robert Warren. 1997. "Socioeconomic Indexes for Occupations: A Review, Update, and Critique." *Sociological Methodology* 27: 177–298.

Hayes, Dennis and Robin Wynyard, eds. 2002. *The McDonaldization of Higher Education*. Westport, CT and London: Bergin and Garvey.

Hefler, Jan. 2010. "Former UMDNJ Dean Gets $60,000 Settlement in Discrimination Claim." *The Inquirer* (August 24).

Heisel, William. 2005. "UCI Cardiology Heads Uncertified." *Orange County Register* (December 22).

Heyboer, Kelly. 1999. "Three Newark Universities to Pool Graduate Research." *Star Ledger* (February 9).

——. 2011. "UMDNJ Appoints Robert Johnson as Permanent Dean of Newark Medical School." *Star Ledger* (March 16).

Heyboer,Kelly and Ginger Gibson. 2011. "In Task Force Report, UMDNJ Faces Third Call to Merge with Rutgers University in a Decade." *Star-Ledger* (January 5).

Heyboer, Kelly and Josh Margolin. 2005. "UMDNJ School Dean to Give Up Post." *Star Ledger* (July 1).

Heyboer, Kelly and Ted Sherman. 2006. "UMDNJ Packs Away its 'Golden Parachutes': Severance Policies Halted after Study Calls Them Too Much." *Star Ledger* (February 22).

Heyboer, Kelly and Angela Stewart. 2002. "UMDNJ Battles Plan to Unite with Rutgers – Most at Hearings Bitterly Oppose Idea." *Star-Ledger* (September 19).

Heyneman, Stephen. 2013. "Higher Education Institutions: Why They Matter and Why Corruption Puts Them at Risk." In *Global Corruption Report: Education*, edited by Gareth Sweeney, Krina Despota, and Samira Lindner for Transparency International, 101–107. New York: Routledge.

Hill, Kim Quaile. 2003. "Democratization and Corruption: Systematic Evidence from the American States." *American Politics Research* 31 (November): 613–631.

Houry, Debra. 2013. "College Rankings: A Guide to Nowhere." *Chronicle of Higher Education* (January 28).

Hundert, Edward M. 1996. "Characteristics of the Informal Curriculum and Trainees' Ethical Choices." *Academic Medicine* 71 (June): 624–628.

Ingle, Bob and Sandy McClure. 2009. *The Soprano State: New Jersey's Culture of Corruption*. New York: St. Martin's Griffin.

James, George. 2004. "Interim Chief Named at U.M.D.N.J.". *New York Times* (February 22).

Jenkins, Patrick. 1991. "Pact Gives Stockton Students a Foot in the UMDNJ Door." *Star Ledger* (October 13).

Jensen, Michael C. 2001. "Paying People to Lie: The Truth about the Budgeting Process." Harvard NOM Research Paper No. 01-03 and HBS Working Paper No. 01-072. http://dx.doi.or/10.2139/ssm.267651.

Johnson, Linda. 2007. "Report Says UMDNJ Dean in Camden Changed Grades." *Hispanic Outlook in Higher Education* (November 5).

Johnson, Roberta Ann. 2003. *Whistleblowing: When it Works – And Why*. Boulder, CO: Lynne Rienner.

Johnston, Michael. 1996. "The Search for Definitions: The Vitality of Politics and the Issue of Corruption." *International Social Science Journal* 48 (September): 321–335.

Joint Analysis and Response to the Kean Commission Task Force Report. 2011. *Analysis of Task Force Report-07.13.11*. http://www.aaupumdnj.org/AAUP2010/joomla/index.php?option=co.

Jones, Gail Ferguson. 2011. "Opposing Views: Rutgers' Gain from Med School Merger Would Be UMDNJ's Loss." *NewBrunswickPress.com* (January 12). http://thealternativepress.com/articles/opposing-views-rutgers-gain-fr.

Kastor, John A. 2004. *Governance of Teaching Hospitals: Turmoil at Penn and Hopkins*. Baltimore: Johns Hopkins University Press.

Kaysen, Ronda. 2013. "Glassboro, N.J., Gambles on a University Partnership." *New York Times* (July 17).

Kean, Thomas L. 2010. *The Report of the Governor's Task Force on Higher Education*. Trenton, NJ: State of New Jersey.

Kelderman, Eric. 2012. "North Dakota's Moment in the Spotlight Isn't a Pretty One." *Chronicle of Higher Education* (March 4). http://chronicle.com/article/North-Dakota-Moment-in-the/131041/.

Kenny, Katherine. 2013. "Whistleblowing in Banking Organizations and Changes in the Structure of Work." Paper presented at the SSWO workshop. Montreal: McGill University.

Kerr, Clark. 2001. *The Uses of the University*. 5th ed. Cambridge, MA: Harvard University Press.

Kerr, Clark and Marian L. Gade. 1989. *The Guardians: Boards of Trustees of American Colleges and Universities: What They Do and How Well They Do It*. Washington, DC: Association of Governing Boards of Universities and Colleges.

Kinzie, Susan. 2009. "Medical School's Problems Were Worse than Described." *Washington Post* (February 25).

Klitgaard, Robert 2000. "Subverting Corruption." *Finance and Development* 37 (June): 2–5.

Kluger, Jeffrey. 2009. "Is Drug-Company Money Tainting Medical Education?" *Time* (March 6). http://www.time.com/time/health/article/0,8599,1883449,00.html.

Kocieniewski, David. 2006a. "Report Finds Patronage Rife at a University." *New York Times* (April 4).

——. 2006b. "New Jersey Medical School Gives Blatant Lesson in Spoils System." *New York Times* (April 5).

——. 2006c. "Man Leading Medical School is Not Seeking Permanent Post." *New York Times* (December 14).

——. 2007. "Medical School in New Jersey Selects Leader." *New York Times* (March 29).

Kocieniewski, David and John Sullivan. 2006. "In Newark, a Ward Boss with Influence to Spare." *New York Times* (January 16).

Kraiger, Kurt and Anthony Abalos. 2004. "Rankings of Graduate Programs in I-O Psychology Based on Student Ratings of Quality." http://www.siop.org/tip/backissues/July04/06kraiger.aspx.

Kouchaki, Maryam. 2013. "Professionalism and Moral Behavior: Does a Professional Self-conception Make One More Ethical?" Edward J. Safra Working Papers Number 4. Harvard University: Edmond J. Safra Center for Ethics.

Lagerkvist, Mark. 2011. "Christie's 'Retired' Budget Guru Pockets $1M in Public Payouts." *New Jersey Watchdog* (November 14). http://newjersey.watchdog.org/2011/11/14/goetting/.

Lane, Jason E. 2007. "The Spider Web of Oversight: An Analysis of External Oversight of Higher Education." *Journal of Higher Education* 78 (November/December): 615–644.

Lea, Russ. 2010. "BP Corporate R&D, and the University." *Academe* (November–December): 20–21.

Leatherman, Courtney. 1999. "Federal Lawsuit Charges U. of Chicago with Overbilling Medicare and Medicaid." *Chronicle of Higher Education* (March 25).

Leevy, Carroll M., Earl Phillips, and Stanley S. Bergen. 1975. "The Community and Medical Education: Organization and Function of a Board of Concerned Citizens." *Annals of Internal Medicine* 82 (June): 832–837.

Lehman, Edward W. 2006. "The Cultural Dimensions of *the Active Society*." In *The Active Society Revisited*, edited by Wilson Carey McWilliams, 23–51. Lanham, MD: Rowman & Littlefield.

Leontiades, Milton. 2007. "Rutgers-UMDNJ Merger is Fraught with Peril." *philly.com* (February 5). http://articles.philly.com/2007-02-05/news/25238248_1_higher-educa.

Lessig, Lawrence. 2010. "Democracy after Citizens United." *Boston Review* (September/October). http://bostonreview.net/BR35.5/lessig.php.

Leusner, Donna. 2000. "University Cardiac Program at Risk – Hospital Fights to Keep Unit Open in Face of Competition by Other Facilities." *Star Ledger* (May 14).

Light, Donald W. 2010. "Health-Care Professions, Market, and Countervailing Powers." In *Handbook of Medical Sociology*, edited by Chloe Bird, Peter Conrad, Allen Fremont, and Stefan Timmermans, 270–289. 6th ed. Nashville, TN: University of Vanderbilt Press.

——. 2013. "Strengthening the Theory of Institutional Corruptions: Broadening, Clarifying, and Measuring." Edmond J. Safra Working Papers, No. 2. Harvard University: Edmond J. Safra Center for Ethics. http://www.ethics.harvard.edu.lab.

Light, Donald W., Joel Lexchin, and Jonathan J. Darrow. 2013. "Institutional Corruption of Pharmaceuticals and the Myth of Safe and Effective Drugs." *Journal of Law, Medicine and Ethics* 41(3): 590–600.

Lindstedt, Catherine and David Naurin. 2010. "Transparency is not Enough: Making Transparency Effective in Reducing Corruption." *International Political Science Review* 31 (June): 301–322.

Linhorst, Michael and Patricia Alex. 2013. "Rutgers Board of Trustees Is Safe – For Now." *The Record* (June 28).

Los Angeles Times. 1999. "Panel to Study Problems at Medical School." (November 24).

Lowry, Robert C. 2001. "Governmental Structure, Trustee Selection, and Public University Prices and Spending: Multiple Means to Similar Ends," *American Journal of Political Science* 45 (October): 845–861.

Ludmerer, Kenneth M. 1999. *Time to Heal: American Medicine from the Turn of the Century to the Era of Managed Care*. New York: Oxford University Press.

——. 2012. "The History of Calls for Reform in Graduate Medical Education and Why We Are Still Waiting for the Right Kind of Change." *Academic Medicine* 87 (January): 34–40.

Luthra, Sahil. 2012. "U. Forgoes Action Against Prof after Study Fraud." *Brown Daily Herald* (September 14). http://www.browndaily.com/u-forgoes-action-against-prof-after-study-fraud-1.2762909#.UFc2bkJ8zzJ.

MacPherson, Kitta. 1995. "Cancer Center at Stake as Two Scientists Feud." *Star Ledger* (September 24).

Magee, Joseph C. and Adam D. Galinsky, 2008. "The Self-Reinforcing Nature of Social Hierarchy: Origins and Consequences of Power and Status." ACM 21st Annual Conference Paper. Available at SSRN: http://ssrn.com/abstracts=1298493.

Malone, Tara, Jodi S. Cohen, and Stacy St. Clair. 2009. "University of Illinois Trustee Resigns over Admissions Scandal." *Chicago Tribune* (July 29).

Mangan, Katherine. 2009. "Sick Economy Puts Strain on Teaching Hospitals." *Chronicle of Higher Education* 55 (February 13).

Margolin, Josh. 2005a. "UMDNJ Terms Gift to Group Improper – School to Change Policy on Charitable Donations." *Star-Ledger* (April 20).

——. 2005b. "Paid Adviser to UMDNJ, No Record of His Advice – Stapleton Received $1 Million Over a Decade." *Star-Ledger* (June 14).

——. 2005c. "Codey Taps 2 to Force His Reforms on UMDNJ – Trustees Defied Governor, Left Exec Bonuses in Place." *Star Ledger* (December 20).

——. 2009. "Federal Authorities Quietly Close Probe of UMDNJ Chief Attorney." *Star-Ledger* (July 6).

Margolin, Josh and Kelly Heyboer. 2002. "Kean and Byrne Back UNJ Idea." *Star-Ledger* (October 16).

——. 2005a. "UMDNJ Trustees Awarded Pacts Blindly – Documents Show They Didn't Know Vendors for $149M of Work." *Star-Ledger* (May 5).

——. 2005b. "UMDNJ Let Travel Bills Run Rampant – As Policies Were Bypassed, Staffers Spent Thousands." *Star-Ledger* (June 19).

——. 2005c. "Thief Takes Fiscal Files at UMDNJ-FBI Probers Sought the Records." *Star-Ledger* (August 19).

——. 2005d. "Break-Ins Rampant at UMDNJ Offices – Rash of Burglaries Raise the Suspicions of Federal Investigators Probing School's Finances." *Star-Ledger* (September 10).

——. 2005e. "With Campus Attorney's Exit, a Star Is Done – Lauded as VP, Sanka King Quits Under a Cloud." *Star-Ledger* (December 23).

——. 2006. "Shake-Up, Pink Slips at UMDNJ." *Star-Ledger* (April 26).

Margolin, Josh and Dunstan McNichol. 2005. "McGreevey Backer's $75,000 Deal: Power Broker from Philadelphia Hired by UMDNJ to Serve on Governor's Transition Team." *Star Ledger* (March 6).

Margolin, Josh and Mary Jo Patterson. 2003. "Rutgers Merger Plan Is Mothballed – Politics, Economics and Public Opinion Doom McGreevey's Proposal to Consolidate State Universities." *Star-Ledger* (December 12).

Margolin, Josh and Ted Sherman. 2005a. "UMDNJ Ignored Years of Warning about Overbilling." *Star-Ledger* (December 18).

——. 2005b. "Feds Issue Ultimatum to UMDNJ – Accept Financial Takeover or Face Prosecution, U.S. Attorney Says." *Star-Ledger* (December 21).

——. 2006a. "How UMDNJ Pumped up Its Heart Program." *Star-Ledger* (November 5).

——. 2006b. "At UMDNJ, an Attempt to Cover up $36M Fraud." *Star-Ledger* (November 12).

——. 2006c. "UMDNJ Puts Top Doctor on Leave." *Star-Ledger* (November 22).

——. 2007. "Ex-Worker: UMDNJ Ignored Bad Billing." *Star-Ledger* (October 29).

Master Educators' Guild. Official website. http://meg.umdnj.edu/aboutmeg.htm. Downloaded January 3, 2013.

McGreevey, James A. 2002a. *Executive Order 14*. Office of the Governor. Trenton, NJ: State of New Jersey.

——. 2002b. *Executive Order 42*. Office of the Governor. Trenton, NJ: State of New Jersey.

McGuinness, Aims C., Jr. 1995. *Restructuring State Roles in Higher Education: A Case Study of the 1994 New Jersey Higher Education Restructuring Act*. Denver, CO: Education Commission of the States.

——. 2011. "The States and Higher Education." In *American Higher Education in the Twenty-First Century: Social, Political, and Economic Challenges*, edited by Philip G. Altbach, Patricia J. Gumport, and Robert O. Berdahl, 139–169. 3rd ed. Baltimore, MD: Johns Hopkins University Press.

Meier, K.J. and T.M. Holbrook. 1992. "'I Seen My Opportunities and I Took 'Em': Political Corruption in the American States." *Journal of Politics* 54(1): 135–155.

Middle States Commission on Higher Education. 2010. *Statement of Accreditation Status: University of Medicine/Dentistry of New Jersey*. Accessed May 4, 2010. http://www.msche.org/documents/SAS/509/Statement%20of%20Ac.

Miletich, Steve. 2005. "UW Medical School Failed to Address Overbilling Problems, Panel Says." *Seattle Times* (July 21).

Moran, Tom. 2005. "The Whistleblower: 'I'm No Hero' – To Tell or Not to Tell, That Was the Question." *Star Ledger* (December 23).

Moroz, Jennifer. 2007. "Letter Hints at a Scandal's Tangled Roots." http://www.philly.com/inquirer/special/20070423_Letter_hints_at_a_scandals_tangled_roots.html.

Mumford, Kevin. 2007. *Newark: A History of Race, Rights, and Riots in America*. New York: NYU Press.

Mumper, Michael, Lawrence E. Gladieux, Jacqueline E. King. 2011. "The Federal Government and Higher Education." In *American Higher Education in the Twenty-First Century: Social, Political, and Economic Challenges*, edited by Philip G. Altbach, Patricia J. Gumport, and Robert O. Berdahl, 113–138. 3rd ed. Baltimore, MD: Johns Hopkins University Press.

Murray, Brian T. 1990. "Nurse Group Sues to Block UMDNJ from Joining Undergrad Program." *Star Ledger* (July 17).

Nakao, Keiko and Judith Treas. 1992. "The 1989 Socioeconomic Index of Occupations: Construction from the 1989 Occupational Prestige Scores." GSS Methodological Report No. 74. Chicago: National Opinion Research Center.

Nestle, Marion. 2007. *Food Politics: How the Food Industry Influences Nutrition and Health*, rev. ed. Berkeley, CA: University of California Press.

New Jersey Dental School. 2005. *Bylaws for the Governance of the University of Medicine and Dentistry of New Jersey (UMDNJ)* (July 1).

New Jersey Medical and Health Sciences Education Restructuring Act. 2012. Senate Bill S2063. Assembly Bill A3102. http://www.njleg.state.nj.us.

New Jersey Senate Democrats News Releases. 2006. "Two Senate Democrats Call for UMDNJ Merger Action" (July 18). http://www.njsendems.com/release.asp?rid=1382.

New York Times. 2006. "School for Scandal." (April 9).

Nice, D.C. 1983. "Political Corruption in the American States." *American Politics Quarterly* 11(4): 507–517.

Nicholson-Crotty Jill and Kenneth J. Meier. 2003. "Politics, Structure, and Public Policy: The Case of Higher Education." *Educational Policy* 17(1): 80–97.

Noll, Robert G. and William P. Rogerson. 1998. "The Economics of University Indirect Cost Reimbursement in Federal Research Grants." In *Challenges to Research Universities*, edited by Roger G. Noll, 105–146. Washington, DC: Brookings Institution Press.

Nowlan, James D., Christopher O. Ross, Mildred A. Schwartz. 1984. *The University of Illinois Trustees: "Invisible" Statewide Candidates*. Occasional Papers in Illinois Politics. No. 5. Urbana and Chicago: Institute of Government and Public Affairs.

Nye, Joseph S. 1967. "Corruption and Political Development: A Cost-Benefit Analysis." *American Political Science Review* 51 (June): 417–429.

O'Dea, Colleen. 2012. "UMDNJ Restructuring Plan Finds No Friends in Newark." *NJ Spotlight* (March 7). http://www.njspotlight.com/stories/12/0306/2330/.

OPPAGA. 2010. "Increased Accountability and Oversight of University Centers and Institutes Is Needed." Report No. 10–41 (May). Tallahassee, FL: Office of Program Policy Analysis & Government Accountability.

Orlando, Andrea. 1998. "Medical School Opens Scotch Plains Campus." *Star Ledger* (April 15).

Ornstein, Charles and Tracy Weber. 2011. "Financial Ties Bind Medical Societies to Drug and Device Makers." http://www.propublica.org/article/medical-societies-and-financial-ties-.

Palmer, Donald. 2013. *Normal Organizational Wrongdoing: A Critical Analysis of Theeories of Misconduct in and by Organizations*. New York: Oxford University Press.

Panebianco, Angelo. 1988. *Political Parties: Organization and Power*. Cambridge: Cambridge University Press.

Patterson, Mary Jo. 2004. "The Ex-Priest Finds a Calling – UMDNJ's President Shrugs Off Doubters." *Star Ledger* (November 21).

Pérez-Peña, Richard and Daniel E. Slotnick. 2012. "Gaming the College Rankings." *New York Times* (February 1).

Perrow, Charles. 1986. *Complex Organizations*. New York: Random House.

Pescosolido, Bernice A., Steven A. Tuch, and Jack K. Martin. 2001. "The Profession of Medicine and the Public: Examining Americans' Changing Confidence in Physician Authority from the Beginning of the 'Health Care Crisis' to the Era of Health Care Reform." *Journal of Health and Social Behavior* 42 (March): 1–16.

Peterson, Iver. 2002. "Head of State Medical School Faults McGreevey Merger Plan." *New York Times* (November 9).

Pfeffer, Jeffrey and Gerald Salancik. 1978. *The External Control of Organizations*. New York: Harper and Row.

Pinto, Jonathan, Carrie R. Leana, and Frits K. Pil. 2008. "Corrupt Organizations or Organizations of Corrupt Individuals? Two Types of Organization-Level Corruption." *Academy of Management Review* 33(3): 685–709.

Pizzo, Philip A. 2009. "The Role of Academic Medical Centers and Medical Schools in the Training and Support of Physician-Scientists." In *The Vanishing Physician-Scientist?: The Culture and Politics of Health Care Work*, edited by Andrew I. Schafer, 120–137. Ithaca, NY: Cornell University Press.

Pololi, Linda, David E. Kern, Phyllis Carr, Peter Conrad, and Sharon Knight. 2009. "The Culture of Academic Medicine: Faculty Perceptions of the Lack of Alignment Between Individual and Institutional Values." *Journal of General Internal Medicine* 24(12): 1289–1295.

Prechel, Harland. 2000. *Big Business and the State: Historical Transitions and Corporate Transformation, 1880s–1990s*. Albany, NY: State University of New York Press.

Prechel, Harland and Theresa Morris. 2010. "The Effects of Organizational and Political Embeddedness on Financial Malfeasance in the Largest U.S. Corporations: Dependence, Incentives, and Opportunities." *American Sociological Review* 75: 331–354.

Public Employment Relations Commission. 2009. In the Matter of University of Medicine and Dentistry of New Jersey, respondent, and University of Medicine and Dentistry of New Jersey Council of American Association of University Professors Chapters, charging party. State of New Jersey: Hearing Examiner.

Quinn, William T. 1998. "Doctor Says UMDNJ Duped Him on Loan – Countersuit Challenges Terms of Relocation." *Star Ledger* (May 17).

Ragonese, Lawrence. 2003. "Officials at Odds over UMDNJ Nomination – Senator Is Blocking Pick by McGreevy." *Star Ledger* (October 16).

Rapport, George C. 1961. *The Statesman and the Boss: A Study of American Political Leadership Exemplified by Woodrow Wilson and Frank Hague*. New York: Vantage Press.

Reisinger, Sue. 2006. "Casualty of Deferred Prosecution; Did UMDNJ's General Counsel Take the Fall for the School's Administrators?" *New Jersey Law Journal* 23 (October).

Residentphysician. 2009. NIH Awards for 2005. Accessed November 20. http://residentphysician.com/Surgery_rankings.htm and /Pediatrics_rankings.htm.

Review, Planning and Implementation Steering Committee. 2004. (Steering Committee) *New Jersey System of Public Research Universities System Planning Project*. Trenton, NJ.

Riccards, Michael P. 2012a. "Public Corruption in New Jersey Revisited." Hall Institute of Public Policy – New Jersey. http://hallnj.org/topics/42-new-jersey-politics/1441-public-corruption.

———. 2012b. "Reorganizing Once Again." Hall Institute of Public Policy – New Jersey (August 24). http://hallnj.org/topics/36-higher-education/1552-reorganizing-once-again.

Richardson, Richard, Jr. and Mario Martinez. 2009. *Policy and Performance in American Higher Education*. Baltimore, MD: Johns Hopkins University Press.

Robertson, Christopher, Susannah Rose, and Aaron S. Kesselheim. 2012. "Effects of Financial Relationships on the Behaviors of Health Care Professionals: A Review of the Evidence." *Journal of Law, Medicine & Ethics* 40(3): 452–466.

Rose-Ackerman, Susan. 1999. *Corruption and Government: Causes, Consequences, and Reform*. Cambridge UK: Cambridge University Press.

Rosen, George. 1980. *Decision-Making Chicago Style: The Genesis of a University of Illinois Campus*. Champaign, IL: University of Illinois Press.

Rutgers, the State University of New Jersey. 2013. http://governingboards.rutgers.edu.

Rutgers Focus. 2003. "Committees Weigh in on Restructuring." http://urwebsrv.rutgers.edu/focus/article/Committeesweigh in on restructuring.

Salancik, Gerald R. and Jeffrey Pfeffer. 1974. "The Bases and Use of Power in Organizational Decision Making: The Case of a University." *Administrative Science Quarterly* 19 (December): 453–473.

Salmore, Barbara G. and Stephen A. Salmore. 2008. *New Jersey Politics and Government: The Suburbs Come of Age*. 3rd ed. New Brunswick, NJ: Rivergate Books.

Sander, Libby. 2010. "Complaints and Compromises Lead to an Abrupt Departure." *Chronicle of Higher Education* (October 13).

Sanford L. Klein, D.D.S., M.D. v. University of Medicine and Dentistry of New Jersey, Robert Wood Johnson Medical School, and Lawrence Kushins, M.D. 2005. 377 N.J. Super. 28, 871 A.2d 681.

Santiago, Katherine. 2009. "UMDNJ to Pay Federal Government $2M in Medicaid Settlement." *Star-Ledger* (June 9).

Scheppele, Kim Lane. 1993. "'It's Just Not Right': The Ethics of Insider Trading." *Law and Contemporary Problems* 56(Summer): 123–173.

Schmidt, Peter. 1996. "States Loosen Control over Management of University Hospitals." *Chronicle of Higher Education* (February 16).

Schmidt, Stuart M. and Thomas A. Kochan. 1972. "Conflict: Toward Conceptual Clarity." *Administrative Science Quarterly* 17 (September): 359–370.

Schmidtleim, Frank A. and Robert O. Berdahl. 2011. "Autonomy and Accountability: Who Controls Academia?" In *American Higher Education in the Twenty-First Century: Social, Political, and Economic Challenges*, edited by Philip G. Altbach, Patricia J. Gumport, and Robert O. Berdahl, 69–87. 3rd ed. Baltimore, MD: Johns Hopkins University Press.

Schwab, David. 1995. "Court Decides UMDNJ Can't Evict Researcher." *Star Ledger* (November 17).

Schwartz, Robert A. 2005. "The New Jersey Medical School: A 50-year Retrospect." *Acta Dermatoven* 14(2): 69–74.

Scott, Gale. 1996. "High Tab for Charity Care Adds Up to Jobless MDs – Dozens Issued Pink Slips as UMDNJ Pares Teaching Staff in Face of Aid Cuts." *Star Ledger* (March 2).

——. 1998a. "Spouse of Former Whitman Aide in Line for UMDNJ Trusteeship – Doctor Would Have Vote for Med School Chief." *Star Ledger* (April 10).

——. 1998b. "UMDNJ Offers Reins to Texan – Presidency Opens Next Month." *Star Ledger* (May 10).

——. 1998c. "UMDNJ Pursues Ex-Official for Debt – Ousted Executive Owes $600,000." *Star Ledger* (March 25).

Scott, W. Richard. 2004. "Competing Logics in Healthcare: Professional, State, and Managerial." In *The Sociology of the Economy*, edited by Frank Dobbin, 295–315. New York: Russell Sage Foundation.

Scott, W. Richard and Gerald F. Davis. 2007. *Organizations and Organizing: Rational, Natural, and Open System Perspectives*. Upper Saddle River, NJ: Pearson Prentice Hall.

Shaw, Marta M. 2013. "Impacts of Globalisation on the Academic Profession: Emerging Corruption Risks in Higher Education." In *Global Corruption Report: Education*, edited by Gareth Sweeney, Krina Despota, and Samira Lindner for Transparency International, 194–201. New York: Routledge.

Sheps, Cecil G. and Conrad Seipp. 1972. "The Medical School, Its Products and Its Problems." *Annals of the American Academy of Political and Social Science* 399 (January): 38–49.

Sherman, Ted. 2005. "'Reformer' Declines Trusteeship at UMDNJ – Orthopedic Surgeon's Conduct at Hospitals Has Raised Questions." *Star Ledger* (November 22).

——. 2009. "Jury Convicts Former Sen. Joseph Coniglio of Extortion and Mail Fraud." *Star Ledger* (April 17).

Sherman, Ted and Kelly Heyboer. 2005. "Codey Tightens Ethics Rules for College Brass – Surprise Order Bans Trustees Who Do Business with Schools." *Star Ledger* (November 17).

Sherman, Ted and Josh Margolin. 2005. "UMDNJ's Golden Parachutes: Documents Show 3 Former Officials Now under Federal Scrutiny Got Lucrative Severances." *Star Ledger* (December 23).

——. 2006a. "UMDNJ Paid $69,000 for One Official's Limos." Newark, NJ: *Star Ledger* (January 25).

——. 2006b. "Cheating Scam Rocks UMDNJ Dental School." *Star Ledger* (May 16).

——. 2006c. "How UMDNJ Pumped Up its Heart Program." *Sunday Star Ledger* (November 5).

——. 2007. "UMDNJ Plans to Discipline Eight Linked to Exam-Copying Scandal." *Star Ledger* (February 16).

Shibayama, Frank A., John P. Walsh, and Yasunori Baba. 2012. "Academic Entrepreneurship and Exchange of Scientific Resources." *American Sociological Review* 77 (October): 804–830.

Shovlin v. University of Medicine and Dentistry. 1998. 50 F.Supp.2d 297. United States District Court, D. New Jersey. April 3.

Silverman, Ed. 2010. "Baylor College Probes Avandia and Ghostwriting." http://www.pharmalot.com/2010/07/baylor-college-probes-avandia-and-ghostwriting.

Simpson, Dick, James Nowlan, Thomas J. Gradel, Melissa M. Zmuda, David Sterrett, and Douglas Cantor. 2012. *Chicago and Illinois, Leading the Pack in Corruption.* Anti-Corruption Report Number 5. Chicago: Department of Political Science, University of Illinois at Chicago.

Slater, Malcolm S. 2010. "Lawful but Corrupt: Gaming and the Problem of Institutional Corruption in the Private Sector." Working Paper 11–060. Harvard Business School.

Smith, Tom. 2008. "Trends in Confidence in Institutions, 1973–2006." Chicago: National Opinion Research Center.

Sparrow, Malcom K. 2000. *License to Steal: How Fraud Bleeds America's Health Care System.* Updated edition. Boulder, CO: Westview Press.

Stafford, Diane. 2010. "Problems at University Illustrate the Importance of a Vigilant Board." *Kansas City Star* (March 28).

Stainton, Lilo H. 2011. "Medical History: UMDNJ's Long Path to Reform." *NJ Spotlight* (May 3). http://www.njspotlight.com/stories/11/0502/2224/.

Stanford University. 2006/2010. "Policy and Guidelines for Interactions Between the Stanford University School of Medicine, the Stanford Hospital and Clinics, and Lucile Packard Children's Hospital with Pharmaceutical, Biotech, Medical Device, and Hospital and Research Equipment and Supplies Industries ("Industry"). Implemented 2006, revised 2010.

Star-Ledger. 1990a. "Contract Talks to Resume Today between Interns and UMDNJ (June 13).

——. 1990b. "UMDNJ Nurses to Join Professional Union" (September 12).

——. 1990c. "Ramapo Seniors Can Advance at UMDNJ" (December 2).

——. 1990d. "Stockton Teams Up with UMDNJ to Offer Dual-Degree Program for Doctors" (October 21).

——. 1992a. "Drew Joins UMDNJ for Dual Degrees" (March 22).

——. 1992b. "UMDNJ Employees Organizing" (February 2).
——. 2003a. "The Auditor – An Inside Look at the Week in New Jersey" (May 18).
——. 2003b. "UMDNJ Staff, Still at Table, Authorizes Hospital Strike" (August 21).
——. 2004. "Uncertainty at UMDNJ" (November 9).
State Commission of Investigation. 2007. *Vulnerable to Abuse: The Importance of Restoring Accountability, Transparency and Oversight to Public Higher Education Governance*. Trenton, NJ: State of New Jersey.
Stein, Garry S. 2006. *Report to the President and Board of Trustees of the University of Medicine and Dentistry of New Jersey*. Hackensack, NJ: Pashman Stein, Counsellors at Law.
Stein, Jeff. 2012. "Weill Dean Remains on Corporate Payrolls, Sparking Debate about Industry's Role in Academia." *Cornell Daily Sun* (November 30). http://cornellsun.com/print/54564.
Stephenson, Matthew. 2014. "On Differing Understandings of 'Corruption'." http://www.ethics.harvard.edu/lab/blog/408-on-differing-understanding.
Stern, Herbert J. 2006a. *First Quarterly Report of the Federally-Appointed Monitor for the University of Medicine and Dentistry of New Jersey*. New Jersey: April 3.
——. 2006b. *Interim Report of the Federally-Appointed Monitor for the University of Medicine and Dentistry of New Jersey*. New Jersey: April 24.
——. 2006c. *Interim Report of the Federally-Appointed Monitor for the University of Medicine and Dentistry of New Jersey*. New Jersey: June 5.
——. 2006d. *Second Quarterly Report of the Federally-Appointed Monitor for the University of Medicine and Dentistry of New Jersey*. New Jersey: September 18.
——. 2006e. *Interim Report of the Federally-Appointed Monitor for the University of Medicine and Dentistry of New Jersey*. New Jersey: September 18.
——. 2007. *Interim Report of the Federally-Appointed Monitor for the University of Medicine and Dentistry of New Jersey*. New Jersey: September 24.
——. 2008. *End of Monitor Report of the Federally-Appointed Monitor for the University of Medicine and Dentistry of New Jersey*. New Jersey: January 3.
Stetten, Dewitt, Jr. 1983. *How My Light Is Spent*. Unpublished manuscript.
Stewart, Angela. 1995. "Citizen Panel Marks 25 Years as Watchdog." *Star Ledger* (June 4).
——. 1998. "Inside Move at UMDNJ - Department Head Chosen Acting Chief." *Star-Ledger* (May 13).
——. 2003a. "Governor Taps Ex-Seton Hall Leader and Lawyer for UMDNJ Board." *Star Ledger* (March 21).
——. 2003b. "UMDNJ Nurses Approve a Strike - Staff Backs Move at County Hospitals." *Star-Ledger* (August 1).
——. 2005a. "Six UMDNJ Training Programs on Critical List – All May Lose Accreditation, and One Faces the End." *Star Ledger* (May 27).

——. 2005b. "Saint Peter's to Cut UMDNJ Ties in Favor of Drexel." *Star Ledger* (June 9).

——. 2005c. "Another Serious Setback at UMDNJ – Accreditation Lost for Heart Practice." *Star Ledger* (July 14).

——. 2005d. "Conflict Concerns Imperil UMDNJ Reaccreditation." *Star Ledger* (August 9).

——. 2005e. "Paid Leave for Ex-Dean Defended – UMDNJ Chief Vows to Seek Respectability." *Star Ledger* (October 20).

Stewart, Angela and Alexander Lane. 2002. "Hospitals' Rivalry Is Likely to Heat Up – Insiders: Competition Fueled Doctors' Dispute." *Star Ledger* (August 11).

Stinchcombe, Arthur L. 1965. "Social Structure and Organizations." In *Handbook of Organizations*, edited by James G. March, 142–193. Chicago: Rand McNally.

Stoll, Malaika. 2004. *Best 162 Medical Schools*. Framingham, MA: Princeton Review.

Superior Court of New Jersey. 2003. Rohit Romesh Arora, M.D., plaintiff, v. University of Medicine and Dentistry of New Jersey; University of Medicine and Dentistry of New Jersey – New Jersey Medical School; University Hospital; Russell T. Joffe, M.D.; and Jerrold Ellner, M.D. defendants. Chancery Division: Essex County Docket No. C-322-03.

——. 2011. George E. Piper, D.O., plaintiff-appellant, v. The University of Medicine and Dentistry of New Jersey, School of Osteopathic Medicine, and Dean R. Michael Gallagher. Appellate Division. Docket No. A-2123-09T3.

Sutton, Robert. 2011. "How a Few Bad Apples Ruin Everything." *Wall Street Journal* (October 24).

Tenbrunsel, A. 1998. "Misrepresentation and Expectations of Misrepresentation in an Ethical Dilemma: The Role of Incentives and Temptation." *Academy of Management Journal* 41: 330–339.

Tenbrunsel, Ann E. and David M. Messick. 2004. "Ethical Fading: The Role of Self-deception in Unethical Behavior." *Social Justice Research* 17 (June): 223–236.

The Record. 2009. "Needed Departure; John Ferguson to Leave HUMC." (June 22).

——. 2013a. "Rutgers' New Links: Massive Merger Is Sausage Making." (July 2).

——. 2013b. "Rutgers and Legacies: Students More Important than Merger." (July 2).

Thompson, Dennis F. 2013. "Two Concepts of Corruption." Edwin J. Safra Working Papers, No. 16. http://www.ethics.harvard.edu/lab.

Tolbert, Pamela S. 1985. "Institutional Environments and Resource Dependence: Sources of Administrative Structure in Institutions of Higher Education." *Administrative Science Quarterly* 30(1): 1–13.

Transparency International. 2001. *Global Corruption Report 2001*. London: Pluto Press.

——. 2006. *Global Corruption Report 2006*. London: Pluto Press.

——. 2013. *Global Corruption Report: Education*, edited by Gareth Sweeney, Krina Despota, and Samira Lindner. New York: Routledge.

Treiman, Donald. 1977. *Occupational Prestige in Comparative Perspective*. New York: Academic Press.

Tsai, Wenpin. 2002. "Social Structure of 'Coopetition' within a Multiunit Organization: Coordination, Competition, and Intraorganizational Knowledge Sharing." *Organization Science* 13 (March/April): 179–190.

Tuchman, Gaye. 2009. *Wannabe University: Inside the Corporate University*. Chicago: University of Chicago Press.

Turk, James, ed. 2008. *Universities at Risk: How Politics, Special Interests and Corporatization Threaten Academic Integrity*. Toronto: James Lorimer.

Tyrrell, Joe. 2000. "Doctor: Whistle-Blowing Cost Me My Job – Robert Wood Johnson University Hospital Reacted to Complaints by Firing Him, Suit Says." *Star Ledger* (June 30).

UMDNJ Master Educators' Guild. 2004. *Faculty Mentoring Recommendations.*

UMDNJ: Research. http://www.umdnj.edu/research/research03_centers.html.

US District Court of New Jersey. 2006. *United States of America v. Wayne R. Bryant and R. Michael Gallagher.*

United States Senate Committee on Finance. 2007. "The Intimidation of Dr. John Buse and the Diabetes Drug Avandia." Committee Staff Report to the Chairman and Ranking Member. (November) Washington, D.C.

——. 2010. "Ghostwriting in Medical Literature." Minority Staff Report. 111th Congress. Washington, D.C.

Van Maanen, John. 1972. *Observations on the Making of Policemen*. Cambridge, MA: MIT Press.

Vaughan, Diane. 1982. "Transaction Systems and Unlawful Organizational Behavior." *Social Problems* 29 (April): 373–379.

——. 1996. *The Challenger Launch Decision: Risky Technology, Culture, and Deviance at NASA*. Chicago: University of Chicago Press.

——. 1999. "The Dark Side of Organizations: Mistakes, Misconduct, and Disaster." *Annual Review of Sociology* 25: 271–305.

Vesterman, William. 2013. "Rutgers, Inc., or How Thorstein Veblen Explains Today's Policies in Higher Education." *Academe* (September–October): 23–27.

Volkwein, James Fredericks and Shaukat M. Malik. 1997. "State Regulation and Administrative Flexibility at Public Universities." *Research in Higher Education* 38(1): 17–42.

Wallace, Warren S. 2008. "Response to UMDNJ's Actions and the Monitor's Report." blog.nj.com/southjersey-impact/2008/07/wallace.pdf.

Walsh, John. 1971a. "Stanford School of Medicine (I): Problems Over More Than Money." *Science* 171 (February 12): 551–553.

——. 1971b. "Stanford School of Medicine (II): Clinicians Make an Issue." *Science* 171 (February 19): 654–657.

——. 1971c. "Stanford School of Medicine (III): Varieties of Medical Experience." *Science* 171 (February 26): 785–787.

Washburn, Jennifer. 2005. *University, Inc.: The Corporate Corruption of Higher Education.* New York: Basic Books.

Weiss, Joshua. 2010. "Medical Marketing in the United States: A Prescription for Reform." *George Washington Law Review* 79 (November): 260–292.

Weinberg, Loretta. 2013. "Questions Remain Over Pay for Rutgers Chief." *The Record* (July 24).

Werlin, Herbert H. 1994. "Revisiting Corruption: With a New Definition." *International Review of Administrative Sciences* 60(4): 547–558.

Whitlow, Joan. 1990a. "'Stress' Sidelines UMDNJ's No. 2 Executive." *Star Ledger* (October 23).

——. 1990b. "UMDNJ Trustees Seek to Start Nursing School." *Star Ledger* (December 14).

——. 1991. "UMDNJ, Newark Activist Defends Payment for 'Troubleshooting' Post." *Star-Ledger* (March 25).

——. 1995. "Practices Being Bought for UMDNJ Network." *Star Ledger* (January 26).

Wiley, Mary Glenn and Mayer N. Zald. 1968. "The Growth and Transformation of Educational Accrediting Agencies: An Exploratory Study in Social Control of Institutions." *Sociology of Education* 41 (Winter): 36–56.

Williams, Darren. 2007. "Troubles Continue at UMDNJ as Former Exec Files Lawsuit." http://diverseeducation.com/article/6843/.

Wilson, Duff. 2009. "Harvard Medical School in Ethics Quandary." *New York Times* (March 2).

Yudof, Mark G. 2002. "Is the Public Research University Dead?" *Chronicle of Higher Education* (January 11).

Zhou, Xueguand. 2005. "The Institutional Logic of Occupational Prestige Rankings: Reconceptualization and Reanalyses." *American Journal of Sociology* 111 (July): 90–140.

Index